MONEY MAKING
MARKETING
FOR CANADIAN$

A Practical Marketing Handbook
For Canadian Business Owners,
Entrepreneurs And Self-Employed
Professionals

By Dave Dubeau
with 10 of Canada's Leading Marketers

Library and Archives Canada Cataloguing in Publication

Dubeau, Dave, 1968-
    Money making marketing for Canadian$: a practical marketing handbook for Canadian business owners, entrepreneurs and self-employed professionals / by Dave Dubeau with 10 of Canada's leading marketers.

"S" in the word, Canadians, replaced by a dollar sign.

ISBN 978-0-9783090-4-6

    1. Marketing--Canada. I. Title.

HF5415.12.C3D82 2009   658.800971   C2009-903307-0

Cover design by Webgrity

April Dew Publishing Inc
202 - 15388 24 Ave.
Surrey, BC, V4A 2J2
www.aprildew.com

This book is dedicated to my lovely wife, Susy and our two children – Amy and Andy.

Ustedes son mi vida y mi razon de ser. Los amo. Papito.

TABLE OF CONTENTS

ACKNOWLEDGEMENT

I would like to thank quite a few people for their knowledge, guidance, and support.

When it comes to marketing, I first got my feet wet learning from Jay Conrad Levinson and his "Guerilla Marketing" books. They have some fantastic "down and dirty" techniques that I ran with when I was starting my first business – dead broke!

I then came across Jay Abraham. Jay's "big picture" thinking really opened my eyes to how business really could be like – not competing on price, but rather being the value-add option with the big ticket price tag. He also taught me about the lifetime value of customers and how to create "risk reversal" in my offers.

From Jay Abraham, I was led to Dan Kennedy. I started to follow Dan in 1997 or 1998 and I have never looked back. Dan's on-going teaching has provided the "glue" that has made some of this marketing stuff "stick" in my mind! He has provided me with many of the strategies, tips, and techniques that I have used to market my own businesses, as well as those of my clients and partners. If you are looking for an on-going marketing education from the best in the world, there is none better than that offered by Dan Kennedy and the Glazer-Kennedy Inner Circle. Check them out at **www.DanKennedy.com**

Bill Glazer has been instrumental in helping me to keep the saw sharp and to learn new and innovative ways to market "outrageously". By belonging to his Marketing Mastermind groups, I have not only been able to keep on the cutting edge of what is working (and what is not), but I have also been surrounded by truly amazing fellow marketers. Being with them has motivated me to do bigger and greater things!

I would like to especially thank my good friend, business partner, client, and mentor "Canadian Rich Dad", Darren Weeks. Darren is like a marketer's dream come true. He understands the importance of marketing, is willing to invest the money needed to get the job done, and he allows me do the job without interference. It is always great working with you buddy! Rock on.

And of course I must extend a Huge Thank You! to all of my co-authors in this book (in alphabetical order):

Sam Beckford,
Robin J. Elliott,
Owen Garratt,
Neil Godin,
Dan "the man" Lok,
Shane Morgan,
July Ono,
DJ Richoux,
Brandon Roe, and
Troy White.

Knowing these people not only enrich me professionally, but personally as well. Thank you so much for your participation and even more so for your friendship.

A special thank you to Regina Minger for all of her help in managing this project and keeping us on schedule to do it in 90 days! Awesome work! Also, thanks to everyone at April Dew Publishing Inc. for their assistance with putting the book together, editing, layout, etc.

FOREWORD BY 'CANADIAN RICH DAD', DARREN WEEKS

I first met Dave Dubeau back in late 2003. I was giving one of my *How to Get Rich in Canada* presentations in Vancouver. Dave had driven there from Kamloops to attend the event. I had just launched a new advertising business, Doorknob Ads (DKA's). Dave liked the idea and became my fourth licensee with the rights for the Thompson-Okanagan area of B.C.

Before we began working together, I asked Dave to take a personality assessment. It showed he was definitely an Action-taker – and that has proven to be very true. He jumped in and started going with the DKA business very quickly.

As he was beginning with the business, Dave and I would talk quite a bit on the phone. After we finished talking about DKA's, he would ask me about how things were going with my seminar business, how my database was developing, etc. That was interesting to me, as no-one else had ever been that curious about it.

Fast forward to 2006. Dave came to me with an idea to start a membership program for my Fast Track event attendees. I get approached all the time by people who want to do business with me or form joint ventures – and 99% of the time the deals don't make sense, or the people aren't serious or passionate about their ideas. But we had a solid track record behind us, so I was open to listening to him.

That little idea quickly became the *Fast Track Inner Circle* membership program, and with 2,000 members across the country, it has now turned into over a million–dollar-a-year business for us.

Shortly after we started the Inner Circle program, Dave started nagging me to try doing one of my Fast Track events in a smaller city. Until then I had focused on doing events only in big cities like Toronto, Montreal, Winnipeg, Calgary, Edmonton and Vancouver. Given the budget I worked with, I knew that I would usually get on average 300 people at each seminar.

I had seen from what he had done with Doorknob Ads that Dave knew a thing or two about marketing. However, I resisted his "smaller city" idea for a long time because I really didn't think it would work.

Being the persistent guy that he is, after about six months, Dave finally convinced me to give it a try.

To make a long story short, with a third of the "normal" marketing budget, and in a town less than a tenth of the size of the cities I usually appeared at, Dave got close to 500 people to come out!

Needless to say I was impressed, and I changed my mind about going to smaller cities. Dave became my marketing director, and I gave him free reign over the marketing for my companies.

In the 3 years that Dave has been "getting derrières in chairs" (as he says) for my companies, we have quadrupled the size of my database, gone from 5 to over 100 employees, and grown to over $100 million a year in gross sales. That is thanks to <u>all</u> of my employees and partners, but Dave Dubeau has definitely played a big role in that growth.

When it comes to marketing, Dave definitely knows his stuff. As I have said at my events numerous times, I think Dave is the best marketer in Canada. The results he has gotten for my company prove it.

I know how much he invests in his own on-going marketing education, as well as getting to know some of the best marketers in North America.

Dave Dubeau and the Canadian marketing experts he has gathered here are the best around.

If you are a small business owner, entrepreneur or independent professional, I highly recommend that you read this book, and most importantly – take ACTION on what you learn.

See you at the top.

Darren Weeks
"Canadian Rich Dad", founder,
www.FastTracktoCashFlow.com

Notes & Thoughts!

A BRIGHT IDEA

INTRODUCTION

Hello and welcome to *Money Making Marketing for Canadians*. My name is Dave Dubeau, and I want to thank and congratulate you for getting your hot little hands on this fine book!

That alone tells me that you are an action taker and very likely to benefit from reading this!

As the "Chief cook and bottle washer" behind putting this book together, I can say that you are in for a real treat.

This is the only book of its kind that I am aware of – designed specifically for Canadian business owners, entrepreneurs and self-employed professionals AND written by Canadian-based writers.

The group of writers I have gathered together for this project are real go-getters who not only write well, but who actually DO what they are suggesting you do. We are not "academics" who work with marketing "theory", nor are we "journalists" who simply report about what other people do. We are in the trenches, day in, day out, putting this stuff to the test – right here in Canada.

Between the 11 of us, we have sold (or helped others to sell) *at least* half a billion dollars worth of products and services. We have helped thousands of other business owners with their marketing and trained thousands more through our collective teachings.

Offline, online, products or services, retail, wholesale, B2B, B2C, small companies and one man operations, all the way up to Fortune 500 clients – you name it, between the 11 of us, when it comes to marketing, we've done it all.

What we teach and show you in the following pages is proven to work – and work WELL – right here in our good old "home and native land".

But before you get too carried away, I think you should be forewarned about who this book will and will not work for:

Who this book *is* designed for:

- Open-minded Canadian business owners (or marketing deci-sion makers), entrepreneurs, and independent professionals who want to grow their profits quickly, effectively, and affordably – in <u>any</u> economic situation. Boom times, bust times – these strategies work in both (and in the in-between times too!).

If you fit the bill, read on, learn and enjoy, because these tactics and ideas work whether…
- you have a service or product based business.
- you work from home, or from an office or storefront.
- you are young, old, of any race, gender, religion, or sexual preference. It doesn't matter.

However, this is definitely not everyone's cup-of-tea.

Who this book is NOT designed for:

- Low-level employees who cannot make marketing decisions.
- Really BIG companies that have more money than brains, and who can buy market share through sheer force of having mega-bucks to throw at any kind of marketing they get sold on. If they throw enough caca against the wall, some of it will stick.
- Small business owners and professionals who want to emulate the "Big" guys and are more concerned about looking slick than making money.
- Advertising agencies, ad sales people, and graphic artists who get off on stringing their clients along for as long as possible with untrackable, unaccountable marketing and advertising in order to make as much money as possible from them before they finally either wise up and realize they are flushing their hard-earned money down the toilet, or they go broke. The same folks, if they are more concerned about winning advertising industry accolades and recognition for creating pretty, clever, or amusing ads that look "cool", don't make their clients any frickin' money! (OK, I went on a bit of a rant there…it shows you what I think of these kinds of people and their evil and dastardly ways).

If you fall into any of those categories, I respectfully suggest you drop this book like a hot potato and run, don't walk, as far away from it as possible. You won't like what you are going to read, and it will challenge the basic fundamentals about business and your trade that you hold dear.

Still reading?

Alright! Hopefully you are in the first group, (or you are in the second group but really want to mend your evil ways. Repent and ye can be saved!)

Let's go on and see how to make best use of this fine resource!

How to use this book:

Skip around a lot! We are all taught to start with chapter one and work our way through to the end of the book. You have my express permission NOT to do that (you are, however, welcome to if you want). Instead, I suggest you take a quick look through the table of contents, see which chapters "float your boat" and interest you immediately, and start with them first.

Then, if you want to, and you have the time, go ahead and read the other chapters too (they are all very good). If you don't, no problem! You will have learned what you needed to learn. Nobody's feelings will be hurt (we can't tell what you've read or not anyway!).

The book is divided into TWO main sections:

The first section focuses primarily on how to get more new clients/ customers/ patients through your door and doing business with you.

The second part of the book concentrates more on maximizing the value of the customers you've already got by getting them to buy more from you, or to buy more often from you.

As this book is a compilation of chapters written by different expert writers, you will see some ideas presented more than once, but in different ways. I left this repetition in for a couple of important reasons:

1. Seeing the same thing presented from different angles gives you a much more complete picture of the whole, rather than a stilted, one-sided view.

2. Repetition is the key to true learning. If you read it more than once, and in different ways, it will stick better.

You may also find that some things that one writer says may slightly contradict what another says. That doesn't mean that either one is wrong; it means that both opinions have validity depending upon the situation. Like they say, "there are more ways than one to skin a cat", and there are more ways than one to get a customer! Take both opinions into account, then take action on the one that you feel most comfortable with.

And finally, I encourage you to use and put into practice what you learn. Don't just read it and think to yourself, "that's nice...maybe someday I'll..." or cop out with a wimpy, "It all sounds good, but my business is unique, my situation is different, and this stuff doesn't apply to me because I'm so special, blah, blah, blah". These strategies do apply to you and your business. You might just have to apply yourself a little to make the connection – but a connection is definitely there.

If you need further assistance or more information, each writer has provided his or her contact information at the end of their respective chapters. Please communicate with them directly for more help. That's what we're here for!

Cheers,

Dave Dubeau

"When your product is good, all that's missing is the marketing, and if you read this book...and follow the simple directions in it.....there will be no more missing pieces to your success."

Steve Chandler
Author of *The Story of You*
www.clubfearless.net

THE BUSINESS GROWTH TRI-POD

The Only Ways Known to Man (this man anyway) About How to Grow Your Business

By Dave Dubeau

A special thank you to Dan Kennedy and Jay Abraham for their wisdom and clarity in teaching me these concepts.

Business really doesn't have to be all that complicated, especially when it comes to growing your company. There are only 3 ways that I know of that any business can grow (and the reason we are in business is to grow it, right? Even maintaining the status quo is growth in a sense since you have to replace the customers you are losing at least at the same speed you are losing them!).

Business Growth Tri-pod

These 3 ways are...

I   Getting more customers.

II   Getting them to purchase more from you.

III   Getting them to purchase more often.

Pretty simple eh? End of lesson… OK, just kidding!

The concepts are simple; the execution is a bit more challenging. If it were easy, everybody would be doing it and we'd all be multi-millionaires by now! On the other hand, it isn't all that difficult either. Most of it is a mental shift of focus rather than learning a whole new set of skills.

Now let's start going through these concepts one by one, starting with everyone's favourite…

I. Getting More Customers

This is usually the first thing that business owners think about when it comes to growing their business and increasing profits – and it is very important. That is why about 75% of this book is dedicated to that topic. All businesses need a steady flow of new customers/ clients/ patients in order to stay healthy and grow.

But unless you are a brand new business without any current or past customers, this should <u>not</u> be where you focus all of your time and energy. I think that each of these "legs of the stool" is equally important, and should be given equal consideration.

Because so much is already included in other chapters about getting new customers, I'm not going to focus on it here.

So, instead, let's take a look at the other two legs of the marketing tri-pod – starting with…

II. Getting them to purchase MORE from you.

Once you have someone in the door of your business, and they have made the decision to purchase from you, you have already overcome the biggest hurdles out there: getting their attention, and then getting them to take action.

Unfortunately many business people stop there, when if they just put a little bit of thought and effort in, they could radically increase the value of the transaction and the amount of profit that goes into their bottom line.

I'm sure you have experienced this yourself in the past. You go somewhere to purchase something, you get in the "buying" mood – and then you end up buying more than you originally planned on. Maybe it has happened to you when you purchased a vehicle and ended up getting a bunch of add-ons, extended warrantees, and upgrades?

Or perhaps you went in to buy one piece of clothing and ended up getting practically a whole new wardrobe.

(This is especially true for me – I really don't like shopping or buying stuff. When I occasionally do get in the mood, I buy lots at once to get it over with because I don't want to go around shopping any more, much to the frustration of my poor, shop-aholic wife).

It is even as simple as going into a fast food place and either getting fries with that, or going for the biggie size of whatever you were buying.

Costco has built an entire business on this! It seems like our house is full of "multiples" of things; we have 8 measuring cups in the cupboard because they came as a set at Costco! You can't buy a small bottle of anything there – it is all HUGE. I'm not sure what we're going to do with 2 gallons of peanut butter , but I'm sure we'll figure it out!

They do a very good job of increasing the size of the transaction (so you spend more) by only offering multiples or extra large portions of what they sell. Usually it is more economical for you to buy it that way, and they end up with slightly lower margins, but much higher volume.

So look at your own business and see how you can make this work for you.

Getting them in the door and in the buying mood is the biggest part of the job; getting them to buy more at that time is relatively easy. All you have to do is give them a good reason to do so, and good value as well.

Again, going back to your business: How can YOU make this concept work for you?

Can you add MORE of the product/ service that you are selling, and BIGGIE size it?

Can you offer different levels of your product or service at different price points, i.e. your "bronze" level, silver level and then gold (and maybe even "platinum") levels? Each offers more bells and whistles and has a higher price point.

The *Fast Track Inner Circle* membership program I run with Darren Weeks has three levels of membership: Gold (at $39.95 per month), Diamond (at $239.95 per month) and Peak Performers (at $1,000.00 per month). Each corresponding level has more value added to it. The vast majority of our members are at the "gold" level, but even with fewer people in them, the profit margin with the higher level groups is much greater for us.

In every customer base, there is a group of people who want the best of the best – and cost is not a concern. How else do you think the car companies can sell high ticket models and cheap economy models as well? Why else do hotels offer deluxe suites as well as econo-rooms?

Different strokes for different folks.

So let's take a look at this from a dollar$ and cent$ point of view.

Let's say, for example, you have a lawn-mowing company (I know – you probably don't, but stretch your imagination a bit and you will be able to make the example apply to your business). You sell a standard lawn mowing service for $100.00 a month (to keep the numbers simple).

You've been in business for a few years now, and you know that, on average, you keep your clients for 18 months. Your lifetime value of a customer is $1,800.00 and your "hard costs" (labour and supplies) is $50 per month, or $900.00 over the lifetime of the client.

Then let's say that with your marketing efforts, you track them and find out it costs you $200.00 to attract a new client.

Take that cost off your Gross net, and you discover that your net profit per client is now down to $700.00.

Now we add on a "New and Improved" Level of service, whereby you add in aeration and twice-yearly fertilizing for your customers. The price for that program is $125/month, but your hard costs on average are only $55/month (to cover the extra labour costs for aeration and yearly fertilizing).

$125/month X 18 months = $2,250 - $990 (hard costs) = $1,260 - $200 client acquisition cost = $1,060 net profit per client. And that makes it a **51% bigger profit** (with only a 25% increase in price)!

Say you get ½ your clients to take the "new" deal, and ½ stay with the old package. You have still increased your NET PROFIT by over 25% with the same number of clients!

Now some business owners have a hard time with this because they think that somehow they are ripping off their customers if they do it. Nothing could be further from the truth! You are providing them with more value.

Think about it. If they are too busy or uninterested to mow their own lawn, why would they have time or be interested in aerating and fertilizing it? That is just another pain-in-the-butt task that they have to think about, do themselves, or find some other vendor to do for them. By offering them that option you are actually bringing much more value to them and making their lives easier and/ or more convenient.

I am the perfect example of an "ideal" customer for this kind of company. I'm about as handy as a foot, and I absolutely hate doing yard work of any kind. I spend thousands of dollars a year to have someone else take care of my yard and make it look pretty. They do the full deal, from weekly mowing, to aerating, pruning, spraying, fertilizing, etc. They do good work, I don't have to think about it, and my wife is happy. Perfect system if you ask me.

And don't forget, your customers don't *have* to take the more expensive option. They can still stay with level "1" service if they prefer. You are just giving them the option to serve them more, if they want it.

And don't think that this just applies to service businesses, because it doesn't. This works for product-based businesses as well (remember the bundling and "biggie" sizing we talked about earlier?).

I'll use my old "Doorknob Ads" business as an example as well. Like most advertising media, I had multiple sizes of ads that my advertisers could choose from, and the bigger the ads got, the more economical they were compared to buying multiple small ads. So, the smallest ads were the cheapest, but the larger ads were less expensive per square cm.

Not only that, but I did everything I could to get advertisers to sign on for multiple issues of the advertising by giving them frequency discounts and even guarantees in order to get them to sign on for multiple editions.

It really doesn't matter what kind of business or service you have, you can get your clients/ patients/ customers to buy more from you. If you are a dentist, you can get them signed up for teeth whitening instead of just a check up. I've even heard of medical clinics adding to the transaction size by promoting flu shots for their patients.

Financial planners can often offer insurance products in addition to their investment products.

You name it, and I'm sure we could find a way to up-grade whatever is being sold. Even in the undertaking business, there are many, many ways that you can spend a lot more money than you originally expected!

My late father's final wishes were to be cremated. I knew there were a bazillion different options for coffins, and price points to boot. But I wasn't expecting the same thing for urns for the ashes. Well, there are, anywhere from a baggie in a cardboard box, all the way up to $2,000 brass urns! Pretty fancy stuff seeing that it is going to be buried forever or sprinkled in the back yard!

O.K., hopefully you see the possibilities of selling more to the customers you already have. Now let's go on to the third leg of our business growth tripod and see how we can...

III. Get Your Customers/ Clients/ Patients To Buy MORE OFTEN.

We've looked briefly at what most of us focus on when trying to grow our businesses: getting more customers/ clients/ patients in the door. It's important, but it is very expensive, and quite a tough job.

We then saw that once we get them in the door and buying something, it is relatively easy (and very profitable) to get them to spend more with us right away. Offer more value at a higher price and a good number of your customers will go for it.

So, now that you have a customer, and they have bought something from you and maybe even upgraded, the next area we want to focus on is getting them to buy more often from you.

It's common knowledge that it is 5 (or 7 depending on whom you talk to) times easier to get a current customer to come back and purchase again than it is to get a new one in the door the first time.

So why do we focus so little of our time and effort on the customers we've already got?

I think it is because we make the dangerous assumption that because they have done business with us once, it is inevitable that they will keep doing so. We figure "Hey, we did a good job of getting them here; we met their needs satisfactorily, so they should automatically come back when they need what we offer again".

After all, that's what most business owners do, right?

WRONG! That *is* what most business owners do...and that is a BIG reason why 80% of them go out of business within their first 5 years!

Just think about your own experiences. Do you feel an undying loyalty to the new restaurant in town that you try one day? How about to your dry cleaner? Your furnace repair company? Your office equipment supplier? Your printing company? Your bank? Your phone company?

If a competing business came around and made you an offer that was hard to turn down, and made it very easy and convenient for you to switch, how much would you think about it before giving them a try? Probably not much.

Chances are there are only one or two businesses you feel really loyal to. And that's probably because you have a personal relationship with the owner or a salesperson.

Here's the bad news: That's how your customers feel about you too!

Now here's the good news: You can change that and create a "virtual iron cage" around them to protect them from being poached by your competition.

Here are a couple of ideas on how to do it:

1. Communicate more often with them.
Here is a list, in order of preference, about how you should do this. The list is not exhaustive, and you should be communicating using a variety of these forms. If you have a small number of clients/ customers/ patients, you should focus on the top levels. If you have more clients, that might not be so practical, and you will use the methods towards the end of the list.
- Personal visits to them. You go to them.
- Personal visits from them. They come to you.
- Personal phone calls from you.
- Personal phone calls from your assistant.
- Personal letters from you (NOT form letters, but hand written notes).
- Letters from your assistant.
- Special occasion notes/ cards for birthdays, anniversaries, holidays.

- Regular monthly newsletter sent by mail.
- Special offers sent by mail.
- Faxes.
- Emails.

2. Give them V.I.P. treatment.

If they are valued customers/ clients/ patients, they should be treated better than someone who just comes in off the street! Give them "first dibs" on special sales and provide client appreciation events, loyalty discounts, preferential treatment, etc.

3. Get them on a continuity program instead of just a one-time sale.

This is one of the BEST ways to keep your clients coming back to you over and over and over again. It is also a wonderful way to provide some stability to your business, instead of suffering from "feast and famine".

What you have to do is determine the "ideal" amount of your product or service a client should have and how often they should get it, and then create "packages" to deliver this.

Now, before you say "that won't work for my business", let's look at it closer with some examples.

Pizza place: Diana Coutu from Winnipeg (Diana's Gourmet Pizza) has a very successful Pizzeria. She also has a "membership" for which her customers sign up, pay a fixed amount every month, and get gift certificates mailed to them. The advantage to them is that they get a BIG discount on their pizza; the advantage to Diana is that she gets a guaranteed amount of money every single month. They sign up for the program, and they are automatically billed every month. So if Diana has 200 people signed up for her $50/month program, she is automatically getting $10,000.00 deposited into her bank account on the first of the month before she ever opens up her doors! How many pizza shop owners can say that?

She also benefits from her customers' loyalty. Do you think they are going to go to Pizza Hut when they have a $75 credit with Diana's place? I don't think so.

Men's Clothing: Bill Glazer, one of my mentors, owned the most successful men's wear stores in his city. He created a "membership" program for his best customers which cost $300 a year and gave them many more special offers, gift certificates, and bigger discounts than "the average" customers received.

Not only did this provide a nice source of income for him (I think he had 300 – 400 people signed up for the program), but it also had some amazing results. Whereas the "normal" customer would come into his store once or twice a year, these members came in an average of SIX times a year (that is 300 – 600% more often!) AND they spent more, on average, when they did come in!

Tree-care: I'm aware of a tree-trimming company that com-pletely revived their business by creating continuity. At first, they would get a call from a homeowner to come prune their trees. They'd go out and do the job and that was it. Then they would wait for the next call and do the next job. It was always "feast or famine" for them.

Then they got smart. They created some on-going services for their clients, including a spring and fall pruning and a summer spraying. Then they took the total cost of the services, and divided it by 12. So if each service was on average $200, and there were 3 services, they took the $600 total, and divided it by 12 to come up with $50. That is what the monthly continuity price would be for that program (and of course they had a variety of programs at higher price points too).

They went back to all of their previous clients and made them this offer. It made their clients' lives easier, because now the job was going to be done automatically AND they didn't have these big bills every time they got a service; instead they had a lower monthly bill. And their trees were in much better shape because they were being cared for properly.

Over half of the clients took him up on the offer. The tree guy was ecstatic! Now he could plan out his and his worker's time much better because he knew in advance what work he had to do. Not only that, but his cash flow was now much more consistent. The first of every month he knew exactly how much money was going to be in the bank.

He was able to cut down on his other advertising because as he got new clients, many of them signed up for the continuity program, and his schedule was filled up!

And I could go on and on about this. Dentists, lawyers, doctors, financial planners, landscapers, advertising sales, etc. etc.

It works for almost any business – all you need is a little creativity to get it going.

So there you have it. The Business Growth Tripod:

- Get more customers/clients/patients in the door.
- Get them to buy MORE from you.
- Get them to buy MORE OFTEN from you.

I encourage you to think hard about how you can more effectively integrate the last two items into your business. It is much cheaper and profitable for you than just focusing on getting more "new" people in the door. It will make your business more money, and make it much more saleable if you ever want to get out of it.

Dave Dubeau began his infatuation with marketing while living in San Jose, Costa Rica. By learning and implementing effective direct response marketing, he was able to take his start-up company from the bottom of the pack to the top three (with over 50 competitors) in 2.5 years.

Upon returning to Canada in 2003 with his Costa Rican wife, Susy, and their two kids, Amy and Andrew, Dave continued to put his marketing skills to good use – first in the field of "Creative Real Estate Investing", where he did "18 flips in 18 months", then with an advertising business, and later as a marketing consultant.

Dave really came into his own as a bona-fide marketing expert when he began working with "Canadian Rich Dad", Darren Weeks. Together they created the *Fast Track Inner Circle* membership program, and Dave eventually became the "Marketing Guy" for Darren's Fast Track group of companies. Dave began a whole new marketing focus for the companies, helped to quadruple the database from 15,000 to over 60,000 event attendees, and helped the companies to grow to $100M in gross annual sales.

Dave is a firm believer in on-going education and he invests tens of thousands of dollars a year going to a variety of marketing conferences, seminars and mastermind group meetings (many through the prestigious Glazer-Kennedy organization).

Dave's company is appropriately called **Results Enterprises Inc**. and is based out of Kamloops, British Columbia in Canada.

If you would like more information about Dave Dubeau and what he does, please visit **www.ResultsEnterprises.com**

FREE Gift Offer! Get over $595.00 in additional marketing and business building special reports, audio CD's and DVD's mailed right to your door. See page 271 for complete details, or visit: **www.ResultsEnterprises.com/gift.html**

Notes & Thoughts!

THE 1-2-3 BLUEPRINT FOR MARKETING MASTERY

By Troy White

Troy White is a very well known direct response copywriter based out of Calgary. I've known Troy since 2007 when we met up at a marketing conference in St. Louis, but I was very aware of him prior to that due to his "Wild West Marketing Conferences" that he held every year.

Troy is one of our valued expert writers for the Fast Track Inner Circle membership program (www.FTICMembers.com).

Troy's 1-2-3 Blueprint is right on the mark. Simple and easy to follow. Enjoy and Implement!

~ Dave Dubeau

I've been very fortunate to learn from the best in the business... multi-millionaires and billionaire-business-builders alike.... **The common theme?** They understand that marketing and advertising success is formed through following the basics – and keeping it simple.

Once you master the core principles, you can move from industry to industry and achieve exceptional levels of success using those principles. This is the reason that you could strip any millionaire of their business, their contacts, and their money and within 3 years, maximum, they would be back to where they were, or chances are, be even more successful and wealthier than before they lost it.

How? **The basics.** They "get" the basics and know those same rules, with a little creativity and a little application and testing, apply anywhere and everywhere. It isn't about the bells and whistles and all the newest "sexy" toys out there that promise great things. Those are fine to test in your business AFTER you have mastered (and fully exploited) the basics of great marketing.

The key is to understand that, and then FIND WAYS to make it apply to your business. This works. It has worked for me and it has worked for every successful person I know and work with. And it will work for you too.

Most business owners I talk to are clueless about advertising and marketing. They usually copy their competition, which is usually THE WORST THING you can do. There is a 99% chance your competitors don't have a CLUE what makes for effective marketing and advertising, so copying them is NOT a good idea. My goal in this chapter is to condense for you the most important concepts, tools, and immediate steps you can take to improve your cash flow and attract as many highly qualified clients as you can handle.

Moving forward, the rules you need to understand:
1. The purpose of your marketing is NOT to showcase your brand, your logo, or your creative company name. The ONLY rule that matters is the entire goal of your marketing campaigns is to make you money.
2. Branding can and will happen as a benefit of profitable growth.
3. Every advertisement or marketing piece you will send out contains an offer (it does not need to be for them to buy something, as it can be for them to take some kind of action like visiting a web page to get something for free).

4. You will learn how to create compelling offers that get them to take action.

5. Each of the marketing campaigns you launch will consist of a minimum of 3 steps. In other words, when communicating with your clients and prospects, you must send at least 3 different pieces to them in order to call it a properly designed campaign (and one that will actually work and help you achieve goal # 1 from above).

6. No more cutesy sayings and vague one-liners that say and do nothing that takes you closer to goal # 1.

7. You will learn how to become a more natural writer, and use those skills to further build on goal # 1.

8. Your personality in your marketing is your greatest asset. Don't hide the fact that you are a real live person, like most business owners do. They try and mask the size of their company by pretending to be a big company. Putting your face and personality front and center in all your marketing will do more for your sales than anything else you do.

9. Effective advertising rarely looks like advertising.

10. Effective advertising stops your ideal customers in their tracks and literally forces them to start reading your ad.

11. Effective advertising always has some form of tracking mechanism in place so you know exactly if it is working, or not.

During my first few years into copywriting, I logged 2,000 hours of writing and studying from the masters (I tracked my hours). Since discovering this thing called copywriting, I have a whole new world in front of me. I see why most businesses struggle. I see why people think marketing doesn't work. I see why most people think advertising is a waste of money. And I see why some companies go on and accomplish amazing things in record time. I have had the privilege to work with some incredible people, from all over the world, including movie stars, bestselling authors, public speakers, inventors, real estate developers and investors, and information publishers. All said and done, there are probably 35 or more industries I have helped, and I have made them millions and millions of dollars in short periods of time.

Why do I share this with you? Because just 7 years ago I had no idea what marketing was or how it worked. Today, I am an internationally-known entrepreneur who has helped thousands of people turn their businesses around. Every week, my articles go out to over 50,000 people spanning the globe. And I absolutely love seeing the look in a client's eye when they hit their first grand slam in marketing. (The pay doesn't hurt either.)

If I can do it, so can you. I failed English in high school and university. But I quickly discovered that real marketing doesn't care about correct grammar. As you will see in this chapter, real marketing breaks many of the rules of correct English. Yet it works... and the results speak for themselves.

The 1-2-3 Blueprint For Marketing Mastery (the blueprint that helps my clients earn the huge returns that they do). This is the system that I would model to the T if I lost it all and had to start over again.

The 3 foundational principles in moving forward with your blueprint are:

1. Start focusing on generating <u>leads</u> – not sales.

2. Starting using systems to convert leads into sales and sales into repeat buyers.

3. Start using measurable marketing in everything you do.

1-2-3 Marketing Blueprint

Step # 1: Generating Leads Vs Sales

By far the biggest mistake entrepreneurs make in their marketing is moving in way too fast for the kill. It's much like dating; the first thing you focus on should not be getting them back to your place into bed. First, you need to warm them up to you. Then they need to trust you. Only then can you move on to other things. (No interest... no trust... no deal).

The FIRST thing you need to do is find your ideal client.

Who in the heck are you selling to? While this sounds simple, I can bet you probably haven't written it down. Most entrepreneurs I talk to have NEVER thought this through. Their most common response is "I sell to *anyone* with money!" WRONG! When you sell to everyone, you sell to no one. The more focused your ideal client profile is, the greater your sales will be.

Who is your ideal client? Be specific here – it is useless otherwise.

What age are they?
Married?
Kids?
Income level?
Hobbies?
Books read?
Passions?
Work? Industry?
Kind of car they drive?
What do they look for in businesses they buy from?
What kind of clothes do they wear after work?

Again, the more specific you are here, the better this will work for you.

Now turn it into a speech <u>that is coming from them</u>. Write it as if they are talking to you and telling you all about themselves, their lifestyle, their problems, their interests, and specifically what kind of help they are looking for that you may be able to provide. Put a name and a face to them to make it very personal... which it should be

"My name is (perfect client's name here), details on them……"

Turn this into a WANTED poster just like below. You can put this in front of you any time you need to write a new promotion, and then write JUST to that person. Your ads will shine, and will be written to the person you should be selling to.

WANTED

Details of who they are and what they look for from life, business, etc.

If you, or anyone else you know, fits this description...
contact Troy White immediately at 403.259.4566 or through
troy@smallbusinesscopywriter.com to receive your *FREE 3 Ways To Grow your Business Report, The Success Formula Book and Turning Your Words Into Wealth training video.*
No catch, just *free* help to grow your business.

Below you will see a sample template for creating your own two step lead generation system. What would entice them into your business for the first time? Maybe they are looking for more information first? If so, a report or booklet would be appropriate for the free incentive to bring them in. Maybe you could offer them something free when they visit your site or store? Find SOMETHING that they would want, and give it to them just for coming in or expressing their interest (again, when you know WHO you are marketing to, this becomes evident).

1. Start recording newspapers, trade magazines, and directories etc your ideal clients are reading. Note the types of articles that run in those publications. You want your lead generating ad to look as much like an article as possible (**editorial style**

ads generate as many as 6 X as many viewers as traditional ads).

2. What information is most useful to your prospects? What is most interesting? Begin working on a 1 to 3 page special report you can use for lead generation. Ideally you hit on the Top 7 Dangers of Hiring a _____, or The 6 Most Important Tips For Improving Your Business _____, or a complete report based on industry research of 10 Industry Trends That Could Help You _____.

3. When you are in your best "sales mode", do you feel differently than normal? How do you get yourself into that mode? I want you to tape record your best sales pitch, speaking either to a real prospect or to a friend or family member. Then have that recording transcribed to text. That is the perfect foundation for your lead generation and follow up text. Advertising is just salesmanship in print (or on the computer screen). Nothing more, nothing less.

This is the advertisement that worked like wildfire for me for two years in the same newspaper:

"Before Painting Your House… Be Warned!"

Your choice on painting your home is a difficult one. How do you know who is going to give you what you need? How do you know who to trust? How to you choose from all the contractors out there? I've just made it easier for you.

No obligation, no pressure - you will receive honest advice and the best value available for your investment. Don't just say yes to the lowest price. Your home is your largest investment you will probably make in your life, make sure the people you are inviting into your home will treat you, and your home, with the respect that's deserved.

Receive a free report I put together for you called **"The Top 10 Things You Need To Ask Before Hiring A Painter"**

This report is yours - I can mail it to you, or bring it with me on our first meeting. This is as fair as I can be. Since we are considering a long term relationship, I don't want to make any mistakes. I don't think you do either!

For your free special report and consultation, without obligation, call Mark Savoie, Savoie Painting **403.710.2929**, savoiepainting@yahoo.ca

" If you're thinking of painting your home this year, call Mark before calling anyone else! Mark was exceptionally professional and completed the job on time and on budget. You have my highest 5 star recommendation. Thanks again Mark.name"

Or another one:

Are YOU Making The Most Out Of Your Customer Relationships?

Announcing a FREE service to help you attract more clients and improve your cash flow.

Calgary, AB - It's a proven fact that up to 63% of your clients will buy elsewhere due to indifference. Learn how to maximize your customer relationships... while improving your bottom line bank balance. Depending on your business, a 5% increase in customer retention CAN mean up to a 95% boost to your year end profits.

To receive your FREE training dvd and 2 marketing booklets (Creative Marketing Tips and Maximum Profits In Minimum Time), all designed to helping find the greatest opportunities to improve your marketing, fill out the form at CreativeMarketingTips.com and everything will be mailed out to you immediately.

Or, if you prefer to leave your name and mailing address via message – leave your details at 403.259.4566.

This is 100% free. There are no sponsored links, no pop-up ads, no banner ads and nothing you have to buy.

Why? Because Business Edge Readers are among the best entrepreneurs I've ever worked with, and this is my way of giving back. (go to the website to find out who I am). See the webpage for Forbes endorsement of this material.

One last thing: in 2006, one of my clients sold 1,175 products in 48 hours during a new launch - - another sold 20,500 books in 24 days, ALL using the techniques you get here for free. Call now. No catch.

Notice a few things:

1. **There's no company name in your headline** – people could not CARE LESS how creative you are with your

company name;　they want to know what you can do for them.

2.　If you are reading the yellow pages, painting section, and you see all those ads looking and sounding the same, and then you see the ad that says "**HEY!** *Before you call any of these other guys – you had better read this one first*" – and it looks like a newsworthy article – would you not read it?

3.　Notice you are raising questions in your ad that they have never thought of, but need to.

4.　Notice it **looks like an article** in the midst of all these ads (articles get 7 TIMES as many readers as advertisements, so make it look like an article!).

5.　**Notice there is a testimonial.** The name was not there as this was the draft ad before the person's name was actually included. This was the ONLY house painter ad that offered PROOF via testimonials.

6.　**Notice you are offering an education.** They can learn about house painting – what they should and should not be doing. All this before they make a decision on who they are going to use.

You then need to deliver to them the freebies or bonuses you promised. At this point, there should be no catch for them to collect on the promised freebies. All we are doing so far is calling out to the ideal client, saying "here we are and here is something you may find interesting (for free)", and collecting their contact information for sending the free-miums. Once you have a database built, USE IT!

Rules Of Lead Generation and Follow Up Letters

Rule # 1: It must have a good headline – and possibly a different font as the rest of the ad

Use All Bold but NOT ALL CAPS – which is difficult to read.

Your ad must stand out visually from other ads (look at the ads in the section you'll be advertising in and make yours look and sound different).

Use either an attention-getting headline or a benefit based headline: "WARNING! STOP! IF YOU ARE ABOUT TO…", or 'the Fastest and Easiest Way To Lose Weight - For FREE", or "How To Win Friends and Win Friends and Influence People".

Rule # 2: You must address the readers – not yourself

Use "normal people talk" not "advertising" talk. Make it sound like a conversation you would have with a prospect the first time you try to get their attention.

Again, your ad must contrast with others in the section – talk like one of them.

Write your ad as if you are talking to only one person. Most ads are written as if they are talking to a group (use words like "you" and "yours". Count the use of "you" and "your" versus "I" and "we" – less than 5% of all words should be "I", "me" or "we").

People looking at ads are typically interested in buying, so always remember you're talking with people who already have a burning desire for your offer.

Rule # 3: Make your display advertisement as long as it needs to be

There is a false belief that you must keep your ad as short as possible. Again, this is false advice from people who have never been accountable for the results they get from their advertising.

The more you tell, the more you sell has always been true – and it always will be.

Always be addressing the benefits of what you provide to them, not the features. List everything about yourself, your business, your product or service and then ask *"so what?"* Do you answer that?

Do you tell them what it means to them? What is in it for them to read your ad and to call or come by your business?

Rule # 4: Find a way to leave them with an emotion after reading your ad

Create a picture in their mind of their new lifestyle using your product or service and enjoying its benefits, thinking how glad they are that they used your service or bought your product.

BY FAR, the biggest mistake made is to not have a call to action. Most people miss this one. You MUST include one. Ask them to take action, such as requesting your report, or getting their free coupon, or booking a free consultation. Make it a limited time offer or a limited quantity or a single day of the week.

Step # 2: Turning Your Leads Into Sales

No matter how great your leads are, unless you have a solid follow up system in place, you won't convert nearly as many as you could. Once the follow up letters are written, tested, and improved , you can send these out as often as possible, and you will know that you can make $xx,xxx every month as long as you are sending out a certain number of letters.

If your letter # 1 converts 10% of your prospects into buyers, letter # 2 converts 5%, and letter 3 converts 3%, you have 18% of your prospects that you can convert to paid clients without having a single meeting or making a phone call – **the letters can do ALL the work.**

So remember, the goal of all these exercises is to build yourself a business system that makes you money month in and month out. It's something you can repeat, grow, or shrink, depending on how much business you need or don't need.

The most powerful way to do your follow-up is through direct mail, email, audio, or video. Until now, they have put up their hands to say they are interested in your offer. You have taken down their contact information and sent them the gift offered. Now you need to get them to buy into your products and services. And a 3 step follow-up campaign is the most powerful way to close the deal.

I don't have enough room here to properly show you how to create follow-up campaigns that work. But I can give you a formula to use throughout.

Have a look at **www.smalldisplayads.com**, and notice the letter there. It sells a $20 special report which converts very well. The formula that I used there is the one you should be using:

Attention – get them to read it right off the bat. The headline you use is KEY and will make or break your success with the follow-up. Some of the best formulas for headlines will be found in... are you ready?... *The National Enquirer* and *Cosmopolitan Magazine*. These have some of the best headline writers in the world, and you had BETTER pay attention to how they write their cover headlines (email me if you want a list of the 100 most effective headlines ever written – my email address is at the end of this chapter). Right under the headline you need to continue with the same thought you used in the headline. Leading to...

Interest – You've got them to stop and read your letter. Now you need to build up their interest and show them you have something that they will want (if you have done your research, targeted the right person, and got them to put up their hands for more information, you know they are interested). Now you have to build on that interest and give them a reason for them to keep reading...

Desire – This is where you introduce them to the most incredible offer they have ever seen. I like to bundle numerous products or services together and offer them a fabulous deal on the bundle (call the bundle something different so they can never compare apples to apples with your competitors). Offer them an incredible guarantee. A price plan. Testimonials from happy clients. Proof that you deliver on your promises. And then...

Action – This is the most important (yet neglected) step in the entire marketing system. Ask them to take action NOW. Give them reasons and incentives to visit or buy right now. Give them every possible reason to trust you. And make sure they understand what will happen if they don't take action NOW.

Not exactly rocket science – but it certainly makes money on demand.

NOTE: If you want samples of any of the above, email me and I will make sure you get samples you can use as templates)

Step # 3: Measuring And Testing

As mentioned previously, you need to track EVERYTHING, noting what worked, what didn't, how well it worked or didn't, exactly what you did, etc. The easiest way to do this is to keep a simple excel spreadsheet (or something similar) detailing everything that has happened. Then it is time to rank the results you've received.

Rank it:

1. stellar success and either brought in a ton of sales, new leads, or positive comments from your customers and prospects.

2. marginally successful – broke even on profits (or made a small profit), got a few new leads or positive comments.

3. not good results at all – lost money or time for nothing, no new leads or sales, no one even noticed you during your attempt.

4. disgustingly bad – big loser, negative feedback and comments, complete waste of time for your business

Rank everything you have done in your marketing campaigns from 1 through 4.

Then separate these into 1's and 2's (the winners) – then another group of 3's and 4's (the losers). The 1's and 2's you are going to do again, the rest you will hold off on for now and revisit them in 6 months or so (things change and what didn't work now may work exceptionally well in 6 months. The internet and society is on warp drive right now so never throw out your test results).

You can even go further into detail and give your honest thoughts on why some things worked and didn't. These notes you make could be worth a fortune to you in 6 or 12 months. Rather than reinventing the wheel, you may find you tested it already but forgot it didn't work or did work.

Now write out how you can make them better, more fun, more exciting, more profitable, more enticing, more powerful, more appealing to the emotions… anything you can think of to make it better. Write it all down!

Post these types of results on a regular basis. Keep them in a marketing results binder and review them monthly or whenever you need new promotion ideas.

With the above example you would definitely want to run ALL the 1's at least one more time a year, test the 2's again, but don't bother running the 3's.

Things To Test

Test only one thing at a time or the test is invalid; the test must be run in the same list or publication as it was initially.

Free samples	Quantity discounts
Method of payments (cash, cheque, credit card, multiple credit card options, purchase orders, extended payments	Method of response: phone, mail, email, web, fax, in-store
Regular envelope vs larger	Live stamps vs pre-printed
Teaser copy on envelope vs none	Window envelope vs regular
Signature in blue ink vs black	Different headlines
Handwriting in margins or spread throughout	1 page letter vs multiple page
Opening paragraph	Change the PS
Font size	Different font
Color vs black and white	Bonus bundles
Deadlines vs no deadlines	

Write as if from you, not from someone else (ie, staff, a spouse, a client, or a supplier).

NOTE: Do NOT ask your friends, family, or co-workers for their impressions on your marketing! They are the worst ones to ask. Either hire a professional, using the templates here as a foundation, or test your campaign to see the real results. I can't count how many times a spouse or employee has completely destroyed the effectiveness of a campaign with their "thoughts about it". Stick with the formula here – it works in the real world! Your best friend's advice doesn't work in the real world... guaranteed!

Once you have a campaign that works for you, keep using it! Don't stop just because you are tired of it. Send it out to every new lead that comes in the door. If it works once, it will work again. That is the beauty of this kind of marketing. You write a direct response campaign using the principles laid out here, you test the results, you try variations of, find a winner, and then keep using the winner as many times and as often as humanly possible.

That is how fortunes are made and how small businesses become big businesses (or at least very profitable businesses, for those who want to keep it small).

A Challenge To You

Don't just read this book, take action on it. This chapter is one small piece of the entire book, but it holds the keys that can make you millions and help you create the business that supports your dream lifestyle. I challenge you to test out my approach in your business. Dedicate the next 6 months to doing only this type of marketing. Try all kinds or things; the weird and crazy ideas usually get you great results. But the ONLY way you will ever know is if you test some of the ideas out.

After 6 months, look at your results, and let me know how they went, good or bad. Not everything you do will work; even the best-of-the-best fail far more times than they succeed. But they fail at a rapid pace, which is why their success seems to come so quickly.

Send me an email or give me a call. Tell me what happens, and I have a free gift for you when you do.

Or, if you just need help getting started, and don't know where to begin, let me know and I will help you get the start you want.

Troy White has been involved in sales and marketing for over 21 years. He has worked with many of the biggest names in business around the world, as well as effectively helped hundreds of small companies grow their businesses and fatten their bank accounts.

Troy's writing has been mentioned on Forbes.com, has been in major city newspapers (i.e. *Business Edge*, *Calgary Sun*, and *The National Post*), in the *Networker News* and *Rising Women Business Magazine* to name a few. Troy has also been interviewed on talk radio shows around North America.

In addition, he writes a weekly newsletter called *Small Business Mastery*, which is read by over 25,000 subscribers weekly. The *Small Business Mastery Newsletter* goes out to the database of direct marketing great, Mr Clayton Makepeace, who earns millions of dollars a year writing sales letters for companies from around the world.

www.responsivedirectmarketing.com ; **www.troysblog.com**
troy@responsivedirectmarketing.com ; Tel. 403-259-4566

Troy has hosted the highly praised *Wild West Wealth Summit* in Calgary for two consecutive years – with glowing accolades from all those in attendance – bringing in trainers, speakers and multi-millionaire entrepreneurs to share their most successful strategies for growing your business fast.

Troy recently won the 2008 Business Leader of Tomorrow Award presented by Business in Calgary and the Calgary Chamber of Commerce. He was also nominated for the 2009 Calgary Business Oscars in two individual categories (only to be beaten by the $2.5 Billion dollar success story, WestJet Airlines).

You will really benefit from Troy's advice. It is practical and immediately usable for any business that wants to attract a better type of client, and sell more at higher prices to their existing clients.

FREE Gift Offer! Get over $595.00 in additional marketing and business building special reports, audio CD's and DVD's mailed right to your door. See page 271 for complete details, or visit: **www.ResultsEnterprises.com/gift.html**

Notes & Thoughts!

Notes & Thoughts!

A BRIGHT
IDEA

MARKETING DANGEROUSLY

By Neil Godin

When I first saw Neil Godin speak I knew he was a man I wanted to know better. He is a very entertaining, fun and <u>wise</u> marketer. His turn-around marketing has worked amazingly well for businesses in recession and during boom times.

His hands-on practical, cheap & effective strategies are perfect if you are tight on $ <u>and</u> willing to think and act outside of the box.

~ Dave Dubeau

My goal for society is one hundred percent unemployment.

I'm serious. I'm a fervent (okay, fanatical) advocate for independent business. Why? Because I believe that dependency on jobs, bosses, and pay cheques is bad for the soul.

My heart goes out – but only part way – to the millions who perform mind numbing, soul-crushing labour in cubicle canyons supervised by bosses whose key credential is their ability to mimic the pathological behaviour of the bosses above them. The symptoms of this social illness are everywhere. People trading time for money – doing work that means nothing to them. Work expanding to fill the time available. The boss mentality. The job mentality.

Now, thankfully, as the industrial age fades away, many of its mindless, meaningless, mechanical jobs are fading away with it. But even the new "knowledge" jobs of the post-industrial economy place people in similar straits. They still hold "jobs with bosses", and when you have a job with a boss, your life is not your own. You literally trade off your autonomy as an adult human being for the relative security of a pay cheque. You become something of an indentured servant. Yes, there are good jobs and good bosses, but for me, the fundamental truth remains.

The alternative? Independent business – of every conceivable kind. Self-employment. Business ownership. Partnerships. Business co-ops. Contract work. Freelance work. Elance work. Ecommerce. Home-based business. Virtual corporations. Independent professionals. Any kind of enterprise where we depend on ourselves, our customers, and our colleagues for our income, rather than on employers.

While most employed people would rather be self-employed, they keep going back and forth to jobs, complaining about the boss every step of the way. I call this phenomenon "the Dilbert Syndrome". The Dilbert cartoon characters (mainly Dilbert, Alice, Wally, and Asok), keep going back to where the pointy-haired boss rules with an empty head, day after day, year after year, knowing they could simply leave. Why do they stay?

Psychologists use the term self-alienation to describe this behaviour. That part of Dilbert's psyche – the part that allows him to keep going back to the scene of this crime against humanity – ignores, denies, avoids that part of his psyche that knows very well that he could and should get out of there. Sadly, in the course of my work as a consultant and trainer with companies of every size and kind, I see this same drama played out in real life – everywhere. Yes, there are good places to work, but most of the workplaces I visit are a toxic wasteland of human suppression and passive aggression. (I receive the Dilbert strip by email every single morning, seven days a week. It isn't very funny. But it is so perfect.)

Okay. Enough of the rant. So, where do we go from here? Well, into self-employment, of course. But there's a catch. While most employed Canadians dream of starting their own business, most of them don't. When they're downsized by one employer they move heaven and earth to find another. Why don't they bring their dream to life? In a word, fear. Fear of failure. Fear of risking and losing the time and money that it takes to launch your own enterprise. Fear of giving up the company pension plan – or part of it, if they leave early. In fact, I've come to believe that the number one cause of business failure is "not starting". In my experience, anyone "could" succeed in just about any kind of business imaginable if only they knew how to make their business fail-safe – which in turn would overcome their fear of starting.

The solution? Knowledge. Because knowledge truly empowers. And in this case, the key pieces of knowledge needed are knowing how to market, how to promote your business, and how to sell. (No, not old fashioned hard-selling, but new-fashioned relationship selling, where you know how to help prospects identify a perfect fit between what you offer and what they need or want, and you know how to help them make a responsible decision to buy from you, here and now.) If business starters had these two key pieces of knowledge, the failure rate among start-ups would drop like a rock. And established businesses would stop failing as well. (Am I still ranting?)

Canadians are just too conservative!

If you run a business, any business, and you want to ensure your success, make sure that the world – or at least your marketplace – is aware of your existence. Here is an example of how to miss the mark by a mile. Driving into the city of Vancouver (I live in nearby Langley), I barely noticed a line of lettering added to the bottom of the soft blue "Welcome to Vancouver" sign at the side of the road. This line of lettering alerts any visitors and residents who have super eyesight to the fact that there is some sort of international athletic event coming to Vancouver. Want to know more? Here, I'll stop the car, and we'll walk over and take a closer look. Uh huh. Now we can read the message, which states: "Host City – 2010 Olympic and Paralympic Winter Games". Wow. The Olympics. Coming to our city. Who knew?

After all the hard work of preparing for the games, the heartaches, headaches, setbacks and injuries (no, not among the athletes, among the taxpayers), the games will be a great success, I'm sure, and will showcase Vancouver to the world. This is all good, but City Hall is certainly missing an opportunity to promote enthusiasm for the games among the locals. And, sad to say, most businesses tend to be equally shy and conservative – just so darn Canadian.

Start Marketing Dangerously

First, let me explain. When I use the term "marketing dangerously", I'm talking about using a bold combination of organic, guerrilla, and attraction marketing to promote your business. By organic marketing, I mean an approach to business in which you grow your traffic and sales by working with and through your present customers and networks, where you avoid the toxic stress of old-fashioned selling and the expensive fertilizer of paid advertising that doesn't produce. By guerrilla marketing, I mean using creative, off-the-wall, inexpensive, and fast-acting ways to promote business. And, I use the term attraction marketing to describe things we can do, such as writing a newsletter or blog, public speaking, hosting educational events for clients and prospects and so on to attract customers to us.

If Vancouver City Hall decided to market dangerously, it would risk offending residents by erecting huge illuminated signs at every gateway to the city proclaiming the games with lights, colour, and action. With the Goodyear blimp overhead (with Goodyear painted out and replaced by the Olympic slogan in blazing, blinking neon) and with the blimp itself doing manoeuvres through giant Olympic rings that were 50 meters tall suspended in the air by giant helicopters. You get the idea.

Cultivate your business with organic marketing

When you set out to grow your business working with and through your present customers and networks, there is an element of real and present danger. This approach requires us to get close, maybe uncomfortably close, to our customers, vendors, and others. For

example, it means going beyond asking for referrals and instead asking for full blown introductions when a customer knows someone who would benefit in the same way they have from doing business with you. It also means not waiting passively and "hoping" that a customer will mention someone they know who needs you. It means systematically "asking" your clients who they know that you should be talking to. And in doing so, it also means explaining to your customers (and people in your networks) why referrals are not enough and why you're asking for a full fledged introduction. Think about it. If you give me a friend's email address or telephone number, and I call them, aren't I making an unsolicited sales call? Yes I am. And will the call be answered with caution if not scepticism or suspicion? "Who is this? And "who gave you my telephone number?" Ouch. You can see why referrals are so seldom asked for or acted upon; they are so uncomfortable for everyone involved. The solution? Ask for introductions, and only call people who have been told who you are and the benefits of dealing with you, and only call them if they want to hear from you. This way, everyone stays in their comfort zones. And your sales rise because of the truth that the best promotion in the world is a customer telling a friend how wonderful you are. That's (a key part of) organic marketing.

You go, guerrilla!

Most of my marketing and sales consulting and coaching clients are strong, growing companies that want to grow stronger, and larger, and faster. But, I also specialize in working with companies in crisis, where for example, it's all over if they don't come up with a half million dollars in deposits on brand new sales within the next thirty days. This is dangerous work. And it's fun. And frightening. And exciting. And challenging. And rewarding. Which is why I'm motivated to keep doing it. And how do we do it? Mainly via guerrilla marketing.

Here's an example: The scene was an office package business, located on the second floor of an office building. The company was going under – fast. Why? Because their advertising hadn't worked. And they were invisible to the outside world (even though thousands of cars travelled up and down the main street below them). I suggested that we put up a 100 foot banner along the second floor balconies telling the world they existed and offering a special deal.

"Can't do that", the owner said.

"Why not?" I asked.

"City Hall", she answered. "signage bylaws won't allow it".

"What?" I replied. "Are we going to let City Hall run your business?" The owner grimaced and shrugged. "Okay", I said, "let's see what we can do".

I picked up the telephone. Called City Hall. Asked for the bylaw officer. Got him on the phone. Explained the situation in detail. Then I asked, "What's the process? If we put up the banner, do your people take it down right away? Or do you wait for a complaint? Or?" I said that we needed to know how much time we'd have if we went ahead and put the banner up.

A long silence. Then he said, "Well, no, we wouldn't take it down unless there was a complaint. And then we'd send a letter".

"All right", I said. 'so it sounds like we'd probably have at least a couple of weeks – even if we got a complaint?"

"Yes", he replied. Then he added, "Actually, you're calling at a good time, because I will be away on a month's vacation after that. So you probably have at least two months".

"Thank you very, very much", I replied, and we hung up. My client stared at me in utter disbelief. The banner went up. Customers came in. And their business was turned around in a matter of days. Thank you, guerrilla marketing.

Here's another example, a turnaround that involved a housing development near Toronto during "the Great Recession" of the 1980's (when I first started doing turnaround work). The scene: Houses sitting empty. No traffic. No sales. But I was full of ideas and energetically threw them out. One of the partners looked at me (very sceptically) and said, "You want to do what?"

"I think we should hang price tags from the chimneys", I repeated.

After a few moments of stunned silence, he replied, "Why not –
I guess?"

Of course we did other things as well, but when we hung those
4x8-foot plywood price tags from chimneys and on porches
everywhere, with the old prices crossed out, and the new prices in
huge numbers, the houses started to sell.

Another developer we worked with was located on a busy
highway but had virtually no signage, thanks to the usual
restrictions. Solution? We parked a moving van on the highway that
ran past the development and put a thirty-foot banner across it so the
world would know they existed. Then we put up hand-made posters
everywhere that said, "buy direct from the builder", and many more
guerrilla marketing moves. And voilà. They sold out in the next few
months, right at the very bottom of the worst recession since The
Great Depression of the 1930s.

Stop selling – and start attracting customers to you!

If I call you, I'm a salesman. If you call me, I'm an expert.
Come on. Say it with me. "If I call you, I'm a salesman. If you call
me, I'm an expert". Got it?

If you haven't got it, this is a good time to get it. The "it" I'm
referring to is "attraction marketing", a safe, comfortable, fast, easy
(and usually inexpensive) approach to growing and sustaining your
business. Again, the idea in attraction marketing is to position
yourself as 'the expert" in your marketplace so that prospects come
to you, rather than you going to them. Yes, of course, "selling" is
still required, as you move through the process and close the sale.
But, this is so much easier when prospects call you first. Is there an

element of danger in this approach? Of course. In order to position yourself as the expert, you must actually be (or become) a genuine expert. That means staying at the bleeding edge of the trends in your industry, and being (or becoming) a walking encyclopaedia of who's who and what's what, so that you are truly the go-to guy or gal and making sure everyone knows it!

Example: Billy Carpenter, Wine Expert. Sommelier. Proprietor of Vin de Garde Cellar Systems in Vancouver, designers and builders of very high quality wine cellars for homes and restaurants (and a brand new marketing client). At our first meeting, Billy said, "We're doing okay, but I'm worried...the phone isn't ringing".

"Then let's get it ringing", I said. And I suggested he host a series of wine and cheese receptions for builders, architects and interior designers in order to get these very important people through his door so they could see his brand new showroom, be exposed to the quality and versatility of his work, and get a taste of his upstairs wine tasting room (Vancouver's only professional wine-tasting facility). Not only would these receptions position Billy as an expert, they would also give him a tremendous "ice breaker" in the form of the invitations that I encouraged him to deliver "by hand" to building sites, where he would simply ask who the builder or general contractor is, and how he could get his invitation to them. He also telephones architects, interior designers, and builders' offices, asking whom he should send the invitations to, and collecting email addresses, allowing him to multiply the size of his data base. Both approaches, of course, got him into sales con-versations that would never have taken place otherwise. The receptions continue to be a big draw. And, of course, his telephone began ringing immediately. And, while his competitors cut prices and complain about the economy, Billy has raised his prices – and now has a hard time keeping up with the work.

Let's redefine success

Using these three "marketing dangerously" approaches can help any business, including yours, to succeed against any odds and in any economy. Why? Because while you're taking risks, your com-petitors are taking cover. Most business people, especially Canadians, hunker down and try to protect themselves during an economic downturn like the one we're recovering from. And this means that you can succeed simply by taking market share from those who aren't using it, exactly as Billy Carpenter is doing.

But let's be clear. When I say you can "succeed", I'm not talking about becoming another Bill Gates or Donald Trump. When I think of "success", I think of a person maintaining and growing their business in a way that keeps them free from financial stress while being able to invest time in the life-work balance that we all strive for and while they achieve whatever other goals they set for themselves. To put it in really simple terms, I define success in independent business as the ability to replace a pay cheque with income from your own business. Do this, and you are a huge success in my eyes. I don't think Bill Gates and Donald Trump are ordinary folk. Instead, my role model would be the woman who starts a thriving landscaping business with nothing more than an old pickup truck and some basic tools and grows it to the point where she has three working partners and three more self-employed people who help out when needed, while she depends on her customers, partners and contractors for her "success",

She is self-managing, self-determined, self-reliant and self-responsible. And, as adult human beings were meant to do, she is flying on her own wing.

As a business trainer and consultant, Neil works with companies of all sizes – in every kind of business and industry. His client list includes Fortune-1000 level companies such as Ford, McDonalds, Shell, KPMG, Subway, ReMax, Dun & Bradstreet, Primerica, and The Royal Bank as well as hundreds of smaller companies. He has been called "a walking encyclopaedia" of sales and

marketing strategies, ideas, how-to's and success stories. His seminars and conference presentations deliver a fresh, invigorating (and entertaining) flow of ideas that lift audience members out of the box that defines their industry, and into a whole new way of looking at and developing their business.

While most of Neil's clients are healthy companies that want to ramp up their sales, he also specializes in working with companies in crisis, where sales always have to be doubled or tripled immediately, at minimal cost. Doing this specialized guerrilla marketing work over the past 28 years has earned him the nickname, The Turnaround Guy®.

Based in Vancouver, Canada, Neil is the host and publisher of *Marketing Dangerously*, a sales and marketing coaching service that delivers "An Idea a Day" to members around the globe. Included are monthly tele-seminars; a huge archive of business-building articles, and audio and video recordings called 'the Idea Vault". He is also author of *Selling in the (Comfort) Zone* (available at Amazon, Barnes & Noble and other outlets).

As a speaker he has presented to more than 300,000 business people from coast to coast in Canada and the United States.

For more information about Neil Godin, visit:
www.neilgodin.com/marketingdangerously.php

FREE Gift Offer! Get over $595.00 in additional marketing and business building special reports, audio CD's and DVD's mailed right to your door. See page 271 for complete details, or visit:
www.ResultsEnterprises.com/gift.html

Notes & Thoughts!

THE MOST IMPORTANT MARKETING SKILL YOU'LL EVER LEARN
Connecting With Your Audience!
By Shane Morgan

Shane Morgan is an astute marketer and copywriter from Vancouver Island. Shane is another fellow I met originally through Glazer-Kennedy and we ended up attending a few different events together.

Initially I hired Shane to do some copywriting for me, and because I was impressed with the results, I invited him to become one of the expert contributing writers for my BC Profit$ membership program – as well as a featured speaker on a series of "How to Thrive in Tough Economic Times" seminars I hosted.

Shane is very good at connecting with his audience – and that is what truly effective marketing is all about.

~ Dave Dubeau

Here it is… the secret to my success! The number one skill you must perfect before your sales and marketing efforts are going to produce great results is the art of connecting with your audience!

Sounds easy, right? Well, the short answer is both a "Yes" and "No". If you know exactly what to do, it's not so hard, but it will require some effort on your part to learn. If you don't know what to do though, it's a lot like stumbling around in the dark until you bump into them by accident.

If you don't know what you're doing in this department, you're likely to bore people, turn them off, or even offend them!

But don't worry. I'm going to show you how you too can learn this most valuable skill and apply it to your sales and marketing! Here's how I first started to learn the art of connection:

1. First, identify the characteristics of your ideal audience member – presumably, this will be your ideal potential customer. Discover their likes, dislikes, personality type, approximate earnings, if they have children, pets, etc. Once you have as much information as you can find, write it all down and then pin it up beside your desk. This is the person you are writing to. This is your ideal customer or client.

2. Use a friendly, conversational tone. Keep it fun and light. Also, don't slow down the flow of your writing with big words or technical terms – keep it simple and easy to read. When you first start writing, just let it all flow out of you. Don't worry about editing or making changes. You can do that later. For now, just focus on communicating your message.

3. Ask them questions or get them involved in free, interactive experiences with you. Use something like best photo contests, requests for success stories, or feature a customer each month or… you get the idea.

One of the best ways to practice the above three steps until you get good at connecting with your audience is to start up a free online newsletter, also known as an e-zine. There is virtually no cost, it's easy to set up, and it's very interactive. There is also very little risk or pressure for you. You aren't selling anything here, so you can focus 100% on learning to connect with your audience. This gets you comfortable communicating to a large group of people, with the connection and intimacy of a personal letter.

In fact, communicating through email is the ideal medium for you to practice with. I recommend sending between 2-4 emails per month. No more than that though, and space them evenly apart, every week or two. Being consistent is crucial. Remember, you're trying to build a relationship here between you and your list members.

Learn how to effectively connect with your audience first and selling will become much easier, whether face to face or in your marketing. Without that connection though, your sales efforts are doomed to fail, so give yourself some time with this first step.

Using Connection For The Purpose Of Making A Sale!

Once you are good at connecting with the people in your e-zine list, the best way to apply your newfound skill to your sales and marketing is by studying the pro's. Who am I talking about? Professional Copywriters. A professional Copywriter is someone who makes a living by writing sales and marketing materials that generate a response, like a sale or someone signing up for a free trial of a new magazine. When it comes to using the art of connection to inspire people to take action, Copywriters are quite simply the best.

These people know something that you don't, and the best way to learn is to read samples of what they have written. By studying their work, you can literally absorb some of their writing style and approach to help you get better results in your own sales and marketing communications. Remember, a sale begins with the first communication you have with your audience. Every communication after that either moves them closer to a sale or further away. That's why learning to connect with your audience is so critical to your success.

Getting Connected With Your Customers/ Clients/ Patients

To give you a better idea of what I'm talking about here, I highly recommend you read *The Ultimate Sales Letter* by Dan Kennedy. This book really gives you a great overview of, not only the individual elements of copywriting used to create winning sales and marketing materials, but also the overall process involved in doing so. There's a lot more to it than just sitting down and writing a letter.

Another great resource is the Internet. Here you'll find works of some of the best Copywriters in the world. Why? Because any top Internet Marketer either is, or uses, top copywriters. There are so many good examples of great sales letters and emails online these days, you'd be crazy not to take advantage of it. You can literally spy on what the professionals are doing for free!

Here's what you do – simply type their name into Google tool bar or go to www.Google.com

Some of my favourites are…
- Yanik Silver
- Joe Vitale
- Dan Lok
- Jeff Walker
- Rich Schefren
- Ewen Chia

Next, print out each of their sales letters that really resonate with you and put them in a file. Now the real work begins…

1. Read, read, and read some more…. Read the sales letters everyday. Pick a time in the day where you can just sit down and read for 30min to an hour. This will help you absorb the style, tone, and feel of successful copywriters.

2. Write them all out by hand. This step may seem painful or even pointless, but it's probably the single most important step. Making copies of these sales letters by writing them out longhand will not only help you absorb their style, tone, and feel, but it will actually LOCK it into your mind and body – secure forever like it was locked up in Fort Knox!

3. Adapt the sales letters to your own business. Now, I'm not suggesting that you copy their sales letters, make a few changes, and then send them out to your lists or even the public. That would probably be considered plagiarism and get you into deep trouble.

What I am suggesting however, is that you adapt what they have written to your own business as an exercise. This really gets your mind thinking on the right track, and you'll probably find it a lot more difficult than you think!

Following the previous three steps will certainly help hone your newfound skill of applying the art of connection to selling. So are you ready to start writing some of your own sales and marketing materials yet? If you've followed the steps, then the answer is "Yes!", but let's start off slowly.

Start off with getting good at writing the following first:

1. Super short lead generation ads like Pay per click, online classifieds, online directory listings, and newspaper classifieds (50 words or less).

2. Medium length lead generation ads such as magazine ads, print "placement" ads, or online reviews, etc. (100-500 words).

3. Long lead generation ads such as full-page print ads, advertorials, and even 1-2 page online "squeeze pages" where your goal is to get new prospects to sign up for your e-zine in exchange for getting something for free, like an ebook, mp3 audio, or similar.

Make sure your ads follow this formula: Connect with your audience first by promising them something that they want. Make sure to present at least one benefit of what it is you are offering. Offer them something for free in exchange for them contacting you. For example, "You'll get this insightful free report when you call…"

This will help you connect with your audience and then inspire them to take action. You'll know if you've done a good job or not by the response you get. Once you get good at writing these types of small ads, you can do the same thing only on a larger scale with the humble one page flyer!

How To Use The Art Of Connection To Get More Customers Using The Humble One Page Flyer...

I'm going to show you exactly how to use your new skills of connecting with your audience to attract more new customers with one of the most under-utilized marketing pieces – the humble one page flyer!

Now, before you get too excited and try to jump in with all six feet, there are four very important questions that you need to find the answers to. I mean it! Don't write a single word until you've answered these questions.

1. **Who do you want?** In other words who is it you want to reach? Your ideal customer, client or...? What are their likes, dislikes and most importantly what problem do they have that your product or service solves?

2. **Who don't you want?** This would be people who waste your time, won't buy from you, or are those you just don't want to do business with. Believe it or not, by choosing the right words you can actually attract the people you want and repel the people you don't want!

3. **What do you want them to do?** When they have finished reading your flyer, what action is it that you want them to take? Pick something, but only one thing. Keep it simple, e.g. "Call 555-5555 today to get your free report about…"

4. **What will you give them in return?** Remember, you are writing this flyer to connect with your ideal potential customer to inspire or motivate them to take action. Decide what you are going to give them if they do what you suggest.

Let me show you what I'm talking about using a hypothetical example: Promoting your Health Food Store.

1. **Who do I want?** Affluent women between the ages of 40 and 60.
2. **Who don't I want?** Broke pensioners, mostly men over the age of 70
3. **What do I want them to do?** Come into the Health Food Store for the first time.
4. **What will I give them in return?** A free sample of a new beauty product, a 30-day 10% discount card, and free health advice.

Now you're ready to start writing! The first thing you want to do is brainstorm the top 5 or more benefits your audience will receive if they take the action you suggest, i.e. what's in it for them if they visit your Health Food Store?

Once you've completed that task, I want you to sit back, relax, and objectively look at all of the benefits you've written down. Put yourself in their shoes and ask yourself, "Which benefits seem the most appealing to you and which ones seem kind of lame?"

Rate the benefits from most appealing to least appealing (1, 2, 3, etc). Your # 1 rated benefit will now become the basis for your headline and the first couple of paragraphs. This will set the tone and theme of your entire flyer.

Example: The top 3 benefits for coming in to the Health Food Store:
- ✓ Get a free sample of an amazing new beauty aid! (free gift).
- ✓ Get a 30 day 10% off all purchases discount card. (save money).
- ✓ Helpful advice from our resident Master Herbalist! (free qualified advice).

So your headline could look something like this:

"Come In Today To Get Your Free Sample Of An Amazing New Beauty Aid That'll Keep Everyone Guessing Your Age!"

For your opening sentence, re-state the information from your headline, but with more details and using a friendly, conversational tone.

Next, write one or two paragraphs about each of your top three benefits (in the same order as you rated them). Really explain to your audience why each of these things are so great, and how these benefits will help make their lives better or solve a problem that they have been suffering from.

Keep everything focused on your audience, their experience, and how what you have to offer will help them! Remember... connection!

As you write, try to put yourself in their shoes. Really feel what they must be feeling as they walk into your store for the first time and present the flyer to one of the helpful staff members. Imagine their excitement as they receive their "First Time Customer" welcome package. Feel it. Exaggerate that feeling and just let the words pour out of you!

Don't worry about what you're writing, if it's any good or not. Just get it all out! You can always edit it later. The important thing is to have positive, upbeat energy and excitement while you're writing. Everything else will fall into place.

Then when you're ready to wrap it all up, you make your closing offer. This will be determined by your answer to question # 3 (the action you want them to take) and question # 4 (what they'll get in return). Always remember to include a deadline too!

Example: *"Come in to our store before Sept 30th, present this flyer to any member of our staff and you'll get a complimentary first time customer's welcome package! (A $49 value, free). It includes: A free sample of an amazing new beauty aid!; a 30-day 10% off all purchases discount card; and our 10 most popular Health Tip Articles by our resident Master Herbalist".*

Put your phone number, address, and any other contact information that might be helpful to your audience and you're done. That's it! You've just learned how to create a one page flyer that truly connects with your ideal audience and has the potential to bring in a flood of new customers. Congratulations!

Testing Your New Skills By Creating A Sales Letter!

Ah, the simple sales letter. Most businesses or entrepreneurs have written one at one point or another, but very few do it well! Let's say, for arguments sake, that you have a group of people who are interested in what you have to offer but haven't yet bought anything from you.

In this hypothetical example number two, we're going to pretend to be a wholesale home décor warehouse trying to sell a new line of lounge chairs to a group of interested retailers by sending them a sales letter. This will make it easier for you to follow along.

The first thing you absolutely must do is collect some information. So, before you write a word, you must know who you're trying to reach and what you want them to do. Let's begin. We already know who we're trying to reach – the members of your group of retailers most likely to buy from you. The people we want to repel are the time wasters and tire kickers from the same group. You know the type – the ones who'll talk your ear off, ask a million questions and never buy anything from you.

What you're hoping they'll do after reading your letter is place an order for 10 new chairs to sell in their retail outlet. And finally, in return for them taking the risk to order product from you for the very first time, you're willing to give them FREE shipping for the first 10 chairs and a guarantee to buy back any of the chairs that don't sell within the first year after placing their order.

Now because you're a wholesale business selling to retailers, we need to come up with 2 different lists of benefits…

1. **Benefits to the retailer:** why they should carry these new chairs in their retail store.

2. **Benefits to the consumer:** so the retailer can immediately see why their own customers would want to buy these chairs from them.

The most obvious benefit to the retailer is to make money by selling the chairs. After all, that's why they're in business, right? Also, their time and resources are important to them, so they'll be hoping that these chairs are easy to sell. In other words, their customers will want them without any poking or prodding. There's nothing worse for a retail store than product that doesn't sell!

Probably the easiest way to come up with the benefits for the end consumer, is to steal them! What I mean by that is to write down all of the "Features" of the new chairs as outlined by the manufacturer and then translate them into benefits. Here's an example:

Feature: New ergonomic design reduces painful pressure points on your lower back. Chiropractor approved.

Translated into a benefit: The world's most comfortable chair helps eliminate lower back pain and can even improve your posture!

Now let's put the letter together…

Headline: Combine your number one benefit to the retailer with the number one benefit to the consumer. You'll get something like this:

"The World's Most Comfortable Chair Practically Sells Itself!"

Opening paragraph: Open your sales letter by painting a picture in the retailer's mind of what it will be like if they bring in 10 of these new chairs to sell. *"Your customers are going to fall in love with these chairs the minute they sit down. You'll have to pry them out of these beauties!"*

Main body text: Write one or two paragraphs for each benefit to the retailer. Then do the same for the benefits to the end consumer (the retailer's customers). Try to keep each paragraph to about 60 to 150 words each. Break them up if you have to. This will make it easier for your audience to read through it.

Testimonials: If you have testimonials from other retailers who have done business with you in the past or testimonials from consumers about the new chair, you're going to want to use them. Pick out the best and put one testimonial between every 3rd paragraph (approx). Use your judgment to ensure it looks good and is easy to read.

Closing: Summarize the letter by restating the number one benefit to both the retailer and the end consumer. Reassure the retailer that ordering from you is quick, easy, and secure. Be sure to include your special offer for first time buyers:

- ✓ Free shipping for the first 10 chairs!
- ✓ Your Unbeatable Guarantee – you'll buy back any chairs that don't sell within the first year after placing the order.

And most importantly, make sure you include a deadline. (*"Order before ... "*). Last but not least, put your order form on the very last page. Make sure it is clear, easy to fill out, and offers as many ways to order as you can supply: fax, email, online, by phone etc.

One last word of advice. Do not, I repeat, DO NOT let your friends or family read your new sales letter. Find an experienced copywriter or marketer to check it over for you. Why? Because your friends and family are probably not part of the group you are writing to, so they won't care, won't be inspired, and will probably be pretty grumpy about it. Trust me on this one.

Here's A Simple Way To Use Connection To Improve Customer Relations!

Of course using your ability to connect with your audience to help you make a sale is important, it's also critical to use it to preserve or even improve customer relations AFTER a sale as well!

Developing the skills to connect with your audience is also ideal for helping you to create, nurture, and improve your relationship with your clients or customers. And here's one way to do this that takes almost no additional effort on your part, since it's just a few words on a piece of paper that you give to your customers on a regular basis: a receipt.

So my question to you is, "What's on your receipts?" If it's nothing but numbers and mind numbingly boring text, you're missing out on a BIG opportunity. To illustrate the importance of what I'm talking about, let me show you what just one or two well-placed paragraphs on your receipts you send to your customers can do:

✓ Reduce your refund rate.
✓ Create a personal connection.

✓ Prevent "Buyer's Remorse".
✓ Re-affirm they made the right decision.
✓ Pre-condition them to buy more from you or buy from you more often.

Let's assume you run a service based business, like being an Accountant. Your receipts are printed out on an 8 ½ X 11" piece of paper and sent to your customers after they've paid in full. Now, we're going to create a few lines of writing that will go out on every receipt. Simple, right?

Before you begin writing, here are some pointers:

✓ Keep it short and sweet.
✓ Be sincere.
✓ Keep the tone and feel positive, appreciative and loving.
✓ Keep the focus on them.
✓ Close by expressing your desire to be of service to them again in the future.

Remember, when using your "powers of connection" to build and nurture your customer relations, there are three main emotions that you want to touch. They are:

Trust – Make sure to reassure your customer that, yes indeed, they did make the right decision by hiring you for all of their accounting needs. Nobody likes to be scammed or ripped off. If you don't reassure them each step of the way, chances are pretty good that they'll start to assume the worst!

Support – A big part of being in any service business is in taking on the responsibility of handling other people's affairs. Let them know what you are doing for them. Remind them if necessary. This will make them feel nurtured and supported. Once they know they are in good hands, they will relax and be happier.

Exclusivity – Everyone wants to feel special. One of the easiest ways to create this feeling in your customers is to let them know that you are choosy about whom you serve. "We don't work with just anybody!" Once they realize this is true, it will make them feel not only special, but clever and lucky to have secured you as their accountant.

If you're having troubles coming up with words and phrases, try this little brainstorming exercise. Take a blank 8 ½ X 11" piece of paper. Now draw a vertical line down the middle. You now have two vertical columns. At the top of the left hand column, write down the word 'trust". Below it, write down any word that makes you think of the word trust or the emotions behind it. Don't think too much, just write down everything that comes to mind.

Now go through the list of words you've just created. In the next column (to the right) try to come up with at least one thing your business does to make your customer feel the same as the word in the first column. Here's an example: Trust = Our 100% customer satisfaction guarantee.

When you are all done brainstorming and writing out your new "Customer Appreciation and Thank You" message, it should look something like this…

"Thank you for choosing Fred and Company for your accounting needs. We really appreciate your support. As always, it's been an absolute pleasure serving you! Please do not send any

money at this time. This is just a receipt for your records of services you have already paid for.

Here at Fred and Company, we pride ourselves on providing great service to a select few! Call us old-fashioned, but we still think that giving you the time and attention you deserve is worth that little extra. We're sure lucky to have quality customers like you and look forward to working with you again in the future!"

Now instead of just reminding your customers how much they've spent with you, your receipts will make your customers feel smart, appreciated, and well cared for. Plus, they'll begin to feel a little closer to you and be more pre-disposed to call you again! All thanks to a few words on a receipt that you were going to send them anyways. All thanks to the power of connection!

The Ultimate Test: Measuring Your Results!

Unless you are already an expert marketer, you may not know how to determine the difference between a good result and a bad result when measuring your power of connection. For example, say the most recent flyer you wrote and sent out generated a 5% sales response. Is that a good result or a bad result? Well, you're about to find out.

Measuring your response rate can be done in two different ways:

1. Response Rate Percentage: This is the percentage of how many people respond versus how many people saw your offer. Example: You write a sales letter to sell a $30 Audio

CD. You send out 1000 letters and get 50 sales. 50 divided by 1000 = 0.05 or 5%

So, is this a good rate of response? Well, if it was sent out to a cold list (people who had never heard of you) it would be down right miraculous. If it was sent to a warm list, it would still be very respectable.

ALWAYS Measure Your Results

2. R.O.I. or Return On Investment: This measures the difference between the money spent versus money received from sales. Using the previous example, if each sales letter cost you a total of 75 cents (printing, envelope and stamp) and you sent out 1000 of them and made 50 sales at $30

each, your ROI would be $30 x 50= $1500 minus total cost of ($0.75 x 1000= $750). So your ROI would be $750.

You just doubled your money. So did you manage to connect with your audience and inspire them to take action? In this example you did. Of course the more important of the two methods is # 2 because in the end, you're in business to make money right?

So now you know the secret to my success as a professional Marketer. Now it's time for you too. So go out there and start writing. Find your audience and connect. It all begins by you taking action today!

Shane Morgan had his first experience as an entrepreneur at age 17 when he started a professional dog training business in Victoria, BC., Canada.

Several years later, after some travelling and various jobs, Shane found himself back in Victoria, where he began a career in commercial art – at first as a sign painter for Vancouver Island's largest outdoor advertising company. Within a short time, Shane had taken over the day to day operations of the company, expanding its clientele.

Shane left the outdoor advertising business to start and run a small commercial art business, where he designed logos, business cards, sales letters, websites and other graphic based marketing materials. He ran this business for about four years before realizing that he'd only created another job for himself instead of a proper business. This was when his advanced marketing education really began.

Since he wasn't sure about his forward direction Shane closed down the commercial art business and embarked on a 9-5 career that gave him plenty of time on the road. He took advantage of this "driving time" by buying and listening to every CD on business, investing, sales and marketing that he could find! Eventually he stumbled into Direct Response Marketing and the art of Copywriting.

Thus began a decade of study and application, building the skills he needed for business by practicing everything he learned and applying it to online marketing. This included selling items on eBay, Information Marketing, creating multiple online newsletters and of course direct response style websites.

That is when Shane found his true calling – as a professional Marketer & Copywriter, helping business owners and entrepreneurs boost both sales and profits!

In addition to providing one-on-one consultations and coaching, Shane recently started a marketing group where he shares his knowledge with the many members and membership levels. To learn more about this exciting group, simply visit the URL below.

www.SmartThinkingMarketing.com

FREE Gift Offer! Get over $595.00 in additional marketing and business building special reports, audio CD's and DVD's mailed right to your door. See page 271 for complete details, or visit: **www.ResultsEnterprises.com/gift.html**

Notes & Thoughts!

Notes & Thoughts!

A BRIGHT
IDEA

HOW TO DOUBLE YOUR PROFITS IN 90 DAYS OR LESS

By Brandon Roe

Brandon Roe is a successful marketing consultant who I have known since 2006 when he was just starting a marketing group in Vancouver, and I was just starting my Fast Track Inner Circle program up and running.

I respected his marketing savvy and we soon started working together. Now Brandon is a Joint Venture partner with me, heading up our Fast Track Peak Performer Marketing Mastermind group.

How to Double Your Profits in 90 days or less is a great lesson in Dan Kennedy's "Message, Market, Media".

~ Dave Dubeau

If you've been in business for a while, you know how difficult it can be to make really good money – not just gross, but actual profit, the stuff you take home after a hard day's work, to spend on family and friends, to invest in your future.

In the words of Michael Gerber, *"a solid profit is the difference between working 'on' your business versus 'in' your business"*.

And yet, so many small business owners and entrepreneurs focus exclusively on the "gross", how much total money they can make. They ignore how much money gets put in their pocket at the end of the day. It's a major issue that can cause burnout, bankruptcy, and all sorts of other problems. And it's something...

That has to STOP!

The fact is, to be really successful, you must focus on the net profit in your business – how much money you're taking home, taking out of the business, putting into other investments, spending on the good things in life. Specifically, I want to show you how to double your profits in the next 90 Days!

The Secret That Isn't So Much A Secret

Perhaps that sounds a little crazy, or "pie in the sky". After all, you've been working in your business and your industry for X number of years and you know that the standard is X percent; if you're in retail, you might get 10 or 20%, premium retail stores can enjoy maybe 40 or even 50%, in computer and electronics businesses 4, 5, or 6% is good, while gas stations operate on a sliver of profit basis.

And you're right. However, today, I'm not going to talk about *your* business specifically. Today, I'm going to introduce you to a new paradigm, a new way of thinking.

I am going to show you how to double your profits in 3 months or less, no matter what business you're in, by leveraging the power of two powerful, but rarely talked about (and even more rarely used) business "mega-strategies".

Once you've seen behind this curtain, you'll never think the same way about business again.

What keeps you up at night... Indigestion boiling up your throat...

What Keeps <u>You</u> Awake?

In my consulting practice, that's one of the first questions I ask because it's so important to helping me figure out how best to produce great results for my client.

And almost inevitably, the discussion of lack of money comes up – usually that there's not enough to pay all the bills.

And it doesn't seem to matter whether they are businesses making $20,000, $200,000 or even $2,000,000 a year. Because it's never about the gross revenue. It's always about the profit. And in almost all cases in which this situation comes up, it is the lack of profit, or the volatility of it, that causes the greatest problem.

I was recently talking with a client of mine who has a fantastic business, with profits of over 50% on most projects, even though he's in the trades business, which is notorious for price-based competition.

He was telling me about a colleague of his who was getting to the end of his rope. He was in the trades as well, and last year, he grossed nearly $2.5 Million, and netted about 100K – a pitiful 4% return. He was working 80-100 hour weeks, never saw his family, never had any time off, was burning out, and didn't know what to do. Most likely, he will burn out completely in the next 2 years, if not sooner.

Technically, he would have been better off if he had just borrowed the $2.5 million, put it into a relatively conservative investment, and made his money that way.

By rights, business should be the highest return investment vehicle available, because you're the one taking all the risk and investing your money, your health, and your livelihood.

How I Run My Business

My business operates at a 60% profit margin, which means that I keep 60 dollars of every hundred after overhead, marketing costs, and staff expenses are taken off.

That's nearly 1,500 percent MORE than the fellow in the previous example. And unlike him, I actually enjoy doing what I do.

Fundamentally, though, this isn't exceptionally hard to achieve. All you need are two things:

1. Smart "direct style" marketing
2. Cooperation with complementary, and even competing, companies with the same types of customers

Over the rest of this chapter, I'll explore these two concepts in more depth on the path to doubling your profits in the next 3 months.

What Are The Hidden Demons That Hold Your Marketing Back

Before I give you the plan to doubling your net profits in the next 3 months, though, it is vitally important to understand the hidden forces that are holding your business back from the highest possible profitability.

ONE: Bad, Stupid Marketing

The truth is, most small business owner's marketing is absolutely, positively horrible. Here are just a few of the biggest mistakes I see:

1. **# 1 Marketing Sin: Being Boring.**
   Most people's marketing is B-O-R-I-N-G. There's no life, no creativity, no uniqueness. In a world where we are bombarded with nearly 40,000 advertising messages a day,

we need to do something to stand out from the crowd and to get noticed. Getting noticed is the first step towards great results.

2. It's not focused on producing results.

Most people do something called "institutional" advertising. That means that everything they do is branding advertising that's meant to create "impressions". It's also a pile of B.S.

Successful marketing means ALL of your advertising is accountable; it ALL has to produce results or else it gets cut out of the marketing plan. If you are going to place an ad in the paper, run a direct mail campaign, or set up a web site, you should be able to track the results quickly and easily, to react quickly to expand what works and restrict what doesn't in your promotion efforts.

3. Too cheap in what marketing to do.

Most business people are much too cheap when it comes to marketing their businesses. They go for the "bulk" mail, when they should be using a real stamp; they skimp on colour in the ad and go straight for black and white; they reward their customers with lousy gifts for high value referrals (or don't reward them at all). The list can go on and on about this. In my consulting practice, it seems half my job is just getting my client to start investing the appropriate amounts on their clients.

For example, a client of mine who does high-end work in the trades industry has, in some cases, paid as much as $10,000 in a referral fee to a joint venture broker just for making an introduction to a big project.

Another client of mine recently bought brand new Apple IPods as a Christmas gift for his best customers – at $150 a piece!

One business advisor colleague of mine regular spends up to $120 USD on every prospect who requests information on his services, sending them everything from Godiva chocolates and digital clocks to cell phones!

These people understand that so-called "expensive" marketing gets the best results! The fact is, the most successful entrepreneurs KNOW to be generous in what they invest, in order to get and retain customers.

4. **Don't understand the fundamental model to great marketing results.**
   One of the biggest reasons why there is so much bad marketing out there is a simple one: *Most small business people and entrepreneurs do not understand the fundamental model that produces great marketing results.*

The truth is, you need three things in place to create great marketing results. It is these three things upon which every business person's and every sales professional's career should be built. They are:

- The Right Message
- The Right Market
- The Right Media

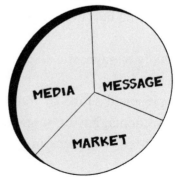

If you put all of these together in the right order, you end up with the RIGHT results.

The most important question in developing your message is this:
"Why should I, [your prospect], choose to buy from you versus the other options in the market?"

The right market is simply a specifically targeted group that shares some common geographic, psychographic (i.e. how they think), or demographic commonalities. Your message needs to be relevant to that market.

The right media is simply the collection of media that appeals to your ideal market. For example, if you are selling weight loss solutions to overweight women, there's a good chance a number of potential customers will be reading *Women's Weekly*. If you want to attract young woman, *Cosmopolitan* magazine might be a good choice for your message. Or, if you want to sell high end clothing to young male professionals GQ might be a good choice.

TWO: Horrible Economics

Another hidden force that destroys many businesses is bad economics. Poor profit margins limit your ability to utilize smart, successful marketing, offer your customers the best service possible, and offer the best quality products.

Oddly enough, it's also often the easiest thing to fix.

I personally love to figure out new "price bumping" strategies for my clients, having worked with them while they increased their prices 20%, 30%, sometimes as much as even 50% or more, without any great client loss. This was money – pure profit – that was just sitting on the table waiting to be picked up.

THREE: Personal Belief Systems

Finally, hidden belief systems stand in the way of optimal profitability in many people's businesses. They have many hang-ups about price, what they think their customers will pay, what they won't pay, why they buy etc.

Often, though, this has nothing to do with reality, but instead is a reflection of the person's own internal conditioning getting in the way.

For example, I worked for a while in an antique store, selling old, dirty pieces of furniture for 20 times what they would have cost new (with new wood, all perfectly put together and flawless). Would I have paid for them? Absolutely not. But I wasn't foolish enough to believe that I was my own customer.

To be really successful in business, and to achieve the greatest profitability possible, you need to be able to constantly examine your personal belief systems about business in general and about money specifically to see if that is what's holding you back.

Now that you have had the chance to find out what could be holding you back, let's now look at what can move you forward.

How To Double Your Profits In 90 Days Or Less

Mega-Strategy # 1:
Switch All Your Marketing Over To Direct Response

When I first started in business, I followed the crowd, did what everyone else did – namely, spending a lot of money advertising and a lot of time praying it would come back. Obviously not a good strategy.

Then, a few years ago, I stumbled across something called "direct response marketing", where I learned that there was a better way that could lead to much better results.

Now, the reason this works so well is simple:

1. **It's got one job: to get excellent results**
    Direct response marketing is designed to get great results, not build a "brand" or "make an impression" or other garbage like that, created by ad agency ad directors who have no earthly idea how to actually sell something.

2. **It's trackable and measurable**
    One of the most beautiful things about direct marketing is its measurability. You can create a campaign, send out the marketing materials, and be able to track where results come from and what types of people are responding as they come in. All this information gives you the opportunity to customize your efforts to only attract the people you want (i.e. those who will pay the higher prices of course), serve only the best customers, and essentially allows you to do business on your own terms.

3. It asks the user to do something

Contrary to popular belief, you are allowed to ask a potential client to do something when reading an ad. Whether you ask them to buy something or simply request more information, the act of encouraging them to respond makes your marketing accountable and a more efficient process.

4. It's based on human psychology

Probably the biggest benefit to using direct marketing in your business is that it's based on basic human buying psychology. Most advertising is creative, meant to win advertising awards, make the owner and the "marketing genius" look good. It's not meant to actually sell anything. The truth is, there are 5 basic stages that people go through when they buy anything, whether it's big expensive things or small cheap things, in business to business settings or selling to consumers. It is:

Step # 1: <u>Awareness of the Need Or Desire</u>

Before anyone is ready to buy anything, they must have a need or desire for it. Before they are in the market for a home, they must want or need shelter. Before anyone will buy a bottle of pop, they need to be thirsty. Before anyone goes for a relaxation massage, they need to be stressed. In some cases, people realize a need. In others, you need to convince them there is a need.

Step # 2: <u>Identification of the Thing That Fulfills the Need.</u>

After the person has accepted that they have the need, they then have to choose the general thing for filling that need. For example, if I have back pain, my options could be:

- Go to the doctor and get a prescription for pain pills

- Take an over-the-counter remedy
- Go to a chiropractor
- Try other natural remedies
- Put a heating / cooling pad on it

… And the list goes on.

The person is then going to pick the thing based on his own personal preferences and experience. If he doesn't like pills, he will probably stay away from the doctor or the over-the-counter remedy. On the other hand, if he thinks chiropractic care or other natural remedies are just voodoo, he'll be more likely to stick with the Western medicine solution.

Step # 3: Identifying why you are the best person to provide the "thing"
This is where your **Unique Selling Proposition** comes in. It's what makes you the best solution for your prospect. Going back to our chiropractor example, let's say that the prospect has decided to go with a chiropractor and is trying to figure out the best option.

He's going to look at the chiropractor's uniqueness, his/her offer, his/her satisfied customers, and then make the decision based on the doctor that is the closest fit to his personal preferences.

Step # 4: Justifying the Price for the "thing"
The next step after you have been chosen to provide the thing is to justify the price for the thing. Most business people do not do anything to justify their price, and so are forced to sit in the middle or lower price point of the market,

never bringing in optimal profits, and being treated as a commodity.

Step # 5: <u>Finding reasons to act now</u>
Human beings love to procrastinate. We can't help it. And when we're selling, we need to realize that and adjust for it. Many sales are lost because business owners simply do not put deadlines into their marketing materials.

Instead, a great potential client sees what you have to offer, likes it, plans to take action – but gets busy, sets it aside, and forgets about the great offer.

At its core, because **direct marketing** is so <u>accountable</u>, so <u>measurable</u>, and is actually based on basic human <u>buying psychology</u>, it **produces much better results than all other forms of advertising and marketing combined.**

However, there is a way to make it stronger, and that brings us to the Mega-Strategy # 2.

<u>Mega-Strategy # 2:</u>
Using Joint Ventures To Explode Your Business

Pretty much any business owner knows that the hardest and most costly expense in a business is getting new customers. Even with the best message, if we aren't targeting the appropriate market, we're not going to get the best results.

That's where joint ventures come in. You see, there are always complimentary businesses out there that cater to the same market as you do. They've already spent the money to bring these customers into the fold – usually a good amount too.

If they are smart, they will want to find a way to leverage that asset as much as possible by introducing complimentary products and services to their base and then taking a cut off any sales made.

That's where you come in. You give them your products and services and let your JV partner offer them to his customer base. They take a cut of the action, and you get new customers.

On the flip side, there are other companies that would love to introduce their products to your customer base. Let them do so and take a cut off the top and commission off the first and all subsequent transactions and watch your profits soar.

It really is true that using these two strategies together can form a powerful alliance that can easily double your profits in 90 days or less.

Here's How To Put It All Together

Phase One:
Ensure the Business Is Already Operating At Peak Efficiency

Step # 1: <u>Identify Your Ideal Target Market</u>
Who is your customer? Where do they live? What do they like? Are they conservative or liberal, Jewish, Christian or Muslim? Are they affluent or middle class?

The first step to doubling your profits is to really <u>get a CLEAR idea of who your IDEAL customer is</u>. Use demographics (i.e. gender, age, family size, income etc), geographics (i.e. where they are), and psychographics (i.e. how they think).

For most of my clients, the ideal client is someone who is willing, ready and able to pay premium prices for a premium version of your service. Just attracting clients like this will already give you a boost to your bottom line.

Step # 2: Create A Powerful Message To Communicate With The Market

Once you have identified who your ideal customer is, you want to create a compelling message that grabs their attention and convinces them to take action and do business with you.

This process all starts with the USP, or Unique Selling Proposition, which is the answer to this question: "Why should I do business with you versus the other options out there?"

As well, an effective message will include proof (such as testimonials), a powerful offer ("FREE" is always a good one, particularly for first time customers who don't yet have a relationship with you), a strong guarantee (always, always worth it), and a deadline to respond (to counteract people's natural tendency to procrastinate).

Step # 3: Choose The Medium

Or media that will communicate your message to your chosen market as cost effectively as possible. This includes such things as newspapers, magazines, radio, television, direct-mail, or any other tool that gets your message in front of your market at the lowest price possible.

Personally, I like the good old-fashioned letter, because it can be used in such a variety of ways, including direct mail and personal letter campaigns, and for joint venture purposes.

Step # 4: <u>Set Up A Joint Venture To Get Your Media Distributed</u>
In my opinion, a joint venture is <u>the most effective way to distribute</u> because it can get your message in front of the PERFECT market with little waste.

When you buy advertising in places such as newspapers, magazines, radio etc, you tend to buy a lot of attention you don't want – people who don't fit into your market and thus have no interest in what you have to offer.

<u>**Phase Two:**</u>
Mine the Value In Your Customer Base

Step # 1: As your list is building, go out and find complimentary businesses (other business that serve the same market as you) that you would feel comfortable in recommending to your customer base. Then, arrange to take a commission off any revenue generated from your customers that go to the other business and distribute their information.

Step # 2: Receive regular commission cheques from your Joint Venture partner.

Step # 3: Have a system in place to periodically check with a few of your customers and ensure that you are getting paid in full by your JV partner.

And that's it!

The Next Step

Go out and double your profits in the next 90 days

Now it is up to *you*. Take what you've learned here and apply it to your own business. Figure out who your target customers are, determine the message that will get their attention, create the materials and go out and joint venture to get your results.
Good luck!

Brandon Roe is a direct-response marketing coach and consultant based in Vancouver, British Columbia, Canada. Over the years, he has worked with numerous clients in over 38 different business industries across Canada and into the US and Europe – ranging from independent service professionals to multi-million dollar retail organizations – helping them to increase their total revenues, improve their profits, and institute marketing systems that automate the inflow of new sales without manual labour.

Brandon is occasionally available for private one-on-one coaching for the right individuals and organizations interested in greater revenue and profit in a shorter period of time.

For a free "'sample" of his service, please contact his office at **info@broeassociates.com**

Notes & Thoughts!

ONE CRUCIAL UNDERSTANDING AND THREE KEY STRATEGIES

By Sam Beckford

Sam Beckford is another "famous-marketer" from the Dan Kennedy world. He began his "brick and mortar" music/ dance school when he rented a classroom from a local elementary school. Through effective marketing and astute business skills, he quickly grew his business to where he now has 3 thriving schools in the lower mainland with over 3,000 students.

In addition to his schools and retail real estate, Sam now trains other music and dance studio owners how to get similar results for their own businesses.

Sam is always on the cutting edge when it comes to marketing, so pay close attention to what he has to share here with you.

~ Dave Dubeau

Marketing is actually pretty boring, but what makes it exciting is how the results can impact your life. In these few pages I'm going to tell you about one specific understanding of marketing and three key marketing that radically changed my net worth and life style. I run a few different businesses. One of them is a music and dance teaching school for kids. To most people, that business sounds like an extended hobby, not a millionaire-maker business. The thing that transformed that "hobby" business into a 2.5 million dollar per year business that makes a solid six figure profit was the correct approach to marketing. Since then I've used my approach to marketing to create another multi-million dollar seminar and consulting business quickly and profitably with practically no risk.

113

One Key Understanding of "Demand"

Marketing is capitalizing on two types of demand for your product or service. I call these two distinctions "Existing" demand and "Created" demand. Surprisingly, most very savvy marketers never address this key distinction. I have looked at and critiqued thousands of ads. I have heard mega best selling book authors and marketing experts give advice without taking this idea of demand into consideration.

What is existing demand? Existing demand occurs when people are looking for your product or service. They already know they want it. They have predetermined that they will purchase it. The only question is *who* they will purchase it from. The last time I flew from Vancouver to Toronto I knew I needed a rental car. It wasn't a matter of "if I needed one", it was just a matter of who I would get one from.

What is created demand? Created demand occurs when you take a product or service and promote it to a market that isn't aware of it or is not aware of their need for that service. They don't know they want it or need it because they are largely unaware of it. When I was building my house I wanted an energy efficient structure. I used a super-insulated concrete building system, used geothermal heating, and even imported some new technologies from the US that weren't available in Canada. I stumbled across a company that did energy "audits" and actually provided professional consulting and measurement to guarantee that your home would be energy efficient to a certain degree.

I was not looking for them; they were looking for me. Once I knew they existed, I suddenly felt that I "needed" their service.

Here's the big problem. Most people selling or marketing take the same approach to sell to both existing demand and created demand customers. In my opinion, the approach you take to sell to someone who knows what they want should be completely different from a person who doesn't know what they want or that you exist.

I have sold millions of dollars of products to both existing demand and created demand markets. Sure, you don't *have* to differentiate your approach to both of these markets, but I promise you will sell more, faster, if you do.

What information should you include or exclude? My belief in marketing is that you want to get to the buying decision as soon as possible. The problem is that the consumer today has too many choices and too much information. Most businesses unnecessarily extend the selling cycle by overdoing it with information.

I've seen websites, direct mail pieces, and brochures that have wasted unnecessary pages telling a story and trying to convince people that don't need to be convinced. I'm not saying that you should not do a thorough job selling and convincing people in your marketing. But if you put too much unnecessary information in front of the prospect, you are costing yourself sales.

This may seem contrary to a lot of marketing information you may have heard. Long letters sell better than short letters; tell them all the merits, don't do a halfway selling job.

So how do you do this? Target your pieces to address either existing demand or created demand prospects. If someone is looking for my service on Google, I want to make the text on my website hit them with the fact that I have exactly what they want.

I want to get to the buying decisions quickly. These days, websites are so cheap that I recommend having multiple websites that either cater to people that are looking for you or people that don't know they need you yet.

Here is an example. If you were selling martial arts instruction, you can get customers who know they want martial arts and they want a provider in a certain area. If they type in a Google search and you come up, your page should acknowledge their search and say:

"Are you trying to decide where to take martial arts in the (specific area) neighbourhood?"

You are answering that one main selling point: "I know I want it, why should I use you?"

Now let's say in that same area you do a Canada Post ad mail campaign to generate martial art students that aren't currently looking for your service. (By the way, one of the gifts we have here in Canada, believe it or not, is the postal system. Ad-mail is cheap to use and can be extremely effective. Check out the Canada Post website.)

The thought of taking martial arts may be the farthest thing from their mind. The copy on your mail piece should therefore be targeted to people that aren't necessarily looking. On that piece you can convince people *why* they need the service. The website they will be directed to can go into detail on why they should take your activity first and then why they should take it from you.

Too many people jump to selling the wrong prospects with the wrong information.

The existing demand shopper knows they want a service and probably knows a ballpark of what pricing should be. You can command a premium price from them if you demonstrate and offer extra perceived and actual value.

The created demand customer may have no idea of what prices should be. You need to educate them with comparables outside your industry first or do a value build up that is not as necessary with existing demand customers.

One of my businesses is doing seminars and consulting. In the last 6 years I have convinced thousands of people to get on a plane and fly to a different *country* to attend my events - not a terribly easy task marketing-wise.

I have sold my events at 3 to 4 times more than close comparisons. My marketing pieces have been very detailed to my created demand prospects and not as detailed to my existing demand prospects.

When someone found me by buying one of my books, the selling process was much easier, but the lion's share of my money was going into the created demand market and explaining and selling to people who didn't know who I was or why they needed me.

Over the years, I've had several people try to copy my seminar business model by offering something very similar at a cheaper price in a more convenient way. None of them succeeded, primarily because they didn't understand the key distinction in selling to existing demand or created demand.

Here's one big tip: You will sell to a larger percentage of your existing demand customers if you keep your message short and targeted. Some of my most expensive, biggest ticket sales have taken 10 minutes – literally. If I had stretched out my marketing and selling process I would have lost sales.

It can take a split second to make a decision to buy a $500,000 house. It can take a millisecond for a person to make a "yes" decision to a marriage proposal.

Existing demand customers know exactly what they want. If a seller tries to over do it by bringing unnecessary details into the equation, the sale will be put in jeopardy.

Think of who you are selling to first, before you decide what you should tell them about your product or service.

There Is A Key Way On How To Think About Marketing

Now here are a few strategies to do:

Use video clips on your website to increase your marketing conversion.

The third most popular site on the internet is YouTube, but most marketers don't use any video on their websites. Video can tell a story better than any sales copy text website or brochure. For the last 2 years I've been using 3-5 minute video "commercials" on a few of my websites to get terrific response. You can check out a couple of my videos at **www.musicanddance.org** to see the promo videos for our music and dance school, or you can see my seminar promotion videos at **www.dancestudiosecrets.com**.

The music and dance school video (musicanddance.org) is more of a soft sell approach that shows more prospects what we do and offer.

The seminar promotion video (dancestudiosecrets.com) is a more hard sell video that convinces prospects to take the next step of requesting information. It has multiple testimonials, a clip of me being interviewed on TV, a writer for Oprah magazine doing an endorsement of my seminars, and multiple shots of the actual events I do. This video sells better than any brochure, web text, or sales letter.

When you are making a video clip, first decide who you are primarily selling to. I like going with 3-5 minutes because you can go into a decent amount of detail without losing a prospect's attention.

Will it take you a bit of work to get a video clip done? Sure, but once you have the clip, you can use it thousands of times to sell thousands of people on your product or service automatically.

Most businesses don't use video on their websites. They argue that it is too complicated and too time consuming to get set up. If these businesses are your competitors, that's great news. Millions of users upload video every day. You can buy camcorders with one button upload to YouTube functions for just $299. I promise the few hours it will take to make a video can be one of the highest payback marketing activities you ever do.

Hyper-targeted testimonial and marketing photos

Another great strategy I have had great success with is using super-targeted testimonials and photos. These days with the cost of colour printing dropping, it is a must to have good quality photos on your ad pieces. We have gone to great pains to avoid using stock photos and instead opt for pictures of our typical customers. You want to make sure you don't use pictures of clip art or just plain text. You want to make sure you have customers of your typical ages, genders and even ethnic groups showing in your ads.

In Canada we have a multi-ethnic market we are selling to, and there's no point making everyone look like they stepped off the set of *Little House on the Prairie* if you are not selling to that demographic group. On the other hand, there is no value in forcing a multi-ethnic photo into your advertising just to show that you are politically correct. Get photos of your typical customers and use them prominently in your advertising. By the way, my Dad is Jamaican and my Mom was Hungarian, so don't send me an email saying how my last comments sound a little racist.

When you are doing testimonials, make sure you use full names of the people commenting and if possible, use photos. If a person likes your product or service, why should they be shy about saying that fact out loud? If I like the *Bourne Identity* movie, I don't care who knows it. If your customers like what you do, ask them to identify themselves fully. Most have absolutely no problem with it. Think about it, people spend hours posting all kinds of facts and opinions about themselves all over Facebook and other internet sites, so they won't be that shy about putting in a good word for what you do.

Ask them to say a good word and identify themselves.

Another key tip: Make sure you have photos that actually show your customers using the product or doing the activity that you are marketing. I am always amazed at how many people show a picture of an empty restaurant or empty dance studio or tool that is not being used in their marketing. Show the thing you are selling in use, or show the result of it being used if that makes more sense.

"Using XYZ Services has saved my company $23,247.98 in costs and increased our profits by 35.89% in just 5 months! I can't say enough about their professionalism and FAST service." Jim Smythmeister - ABC Co., Vancouver, BC

ALWAYS Use Specific Testimonials

Use multiple websites for leads and tracking

A few years ago you were in the dark ages if your business didn't have a website. Now I think you are in the dark ages if you just use *one* website. Websites are so cheap today that you can get different sites set up for different purposes. Even for conventional, local businesses I recommend having multiple websites. If you are a florist, you don't just sell flowers. You could sell bridal floral arrangements, funeral arrangements, Mother's Day bouquets and potentially hundreds of other kinds of flowers. It is very difficult to get one website to come up high on Google for 50 different things. Why not pick 5 or 6 of your most searched requests and make sites specifically for them?

Will this take some work? Sure. Will it make you a lot of money? Yes. Think of your most demanded and searched items and design a site just selling that specific item. If the website has a link back to your main page that's fine but try to focus just on that one thing. Also remember the principle of existing demand: If people are searching you on Google they already know what they want.

Why the internet has screwed up tracking ads for most businesses

Our stats show us that typical local business prospects go to a website 50-85% of the time before calling or emailing for more information. Here's a big problem: If you are a savvy marketer that asks customers how they found you, many will say "internet" when in fact they received a postcard which made them go to the internet first or looked you up on yellowpages.ca before finding your site.

Many marketers think that offline marketing doesn't work any more because everyone is finding the "online". If you only have one website you will never know how people typed your name in. Yes, you can use extensions on your website, but in my real world, experience extensions (go to .com/hgtv) don't really work.

The solution to effective tracking is setting up a web page that is just attached to one specific ad source. If you are in the yellow pages have one website that is just for the yellow pages. If you advertise in a magazine, just have it in that magazine. Is this a bit of work? Sure, but it's smart work. Many businesses will spend $5,000 per year on the yellow pages and then will refuse to spend $200 per year on a simple web site to see how many people are actually responding. This is a small but crucial step. Setting up multiple websites will help you track and sell better. You can also specifically target those sites for existing or created demand users.

So there you go – one key psychological factor and three key strategies. Use them and prosper. I wish you all the best in marketing your way to the life you really want.

After 5 failed business attempts, Sam Beckford started an ordinary small business that has made him a millionaire at age 34. After achieving that success in his own small business, Sam started sharing his ideas with other business owners and has personally helped hundreds of small business owners increase their income by over $40,000 per year while working less.

In 2009 Sam completed construction of his exclusive waterfront coaching center 45 minutes outside Vancouver. The site *Creator's Landing* is a unique setting where he combines information and motivation to help entrepreneurs rapidly increase net worth and semi-retire.

Sam's next book, *The Small Business Wealth Triangle – the ultimate strategy to semi-retire faster, richer and happier* is scheduled to be released in early 2010.

FREE Gift Offer! Get over $595.00 in additional marketing and business building special reports, audio CD's and DVD's mailed right to your door. See page 271 for complete details, or visit: **www.ResultsEnterprises.com/gift.html**

Notes & Thoughts!

Notes & Thoughts!

A BRIGHT
IDEA

THE SMALL BUSINESS WORLD HAS CHANGED FOREVER

Will You Adapt or Die in the New Era?

By Robin J. Elliott

Robin J Elliott's stuff works. I'm living proof of it. I attended one of his seminars in late 2005. I grabbed one of his strategies, applied it and turned it into a $1M plus business venture with Canadian Rich Dad, Darren Weeks – what is now our Fast Track Inner Circle.

Robin's teachings give people a complete "mind shift" and a new way of looking at business.

I asked Robin to provide information about JV strategies for building up an existing business fast, and that is what he shares with us in this chapter.

~ Dave Dubeau

The New Reality

The world has changed, dramatically, and forever. It won't go back to the way it was before the recession. I won't go into detail, since that's not the point. The point is that business will not be done in the same way as it was done before. We have entered a new era of business and money, and savvy entrepreneurs had better get with the new program or end up on the scrap heap with VCRs, 8-Track Tapes, and Commodore 64s. Governments and banks have imposed, and continue to establish, new rules which will require entrepreneurs to use new systems and methods to get rich.

127

This is not bad news; it's just news, and those of us who know that change is a necessary part of business success realize that this wave of change is going to dump a lot of our competition on a rocky beach, while those of us who choose to ride that wave will land gently on Treasure Island, along with our friends. You can't put new wine into old wineskins, and trying to force the old ways into a new system will be like trying to make your iPod play on a gramophone: frustrating, costly, and ineffective – a mere waste of time and money, the very commodities we are in business to create. The world is moving ever faster, and combined with the recent changes, of which many of us are blissfully unaware, we can expect a radical shift in the way we have to do business in order not only to survive, but also to flourish and thrive.

Gone are the days of customer loyalty, effective, low-cost advertising, the hard sell, and manipulative copywriting. Those who were coasting along on momentum created during good times will find the proverbial carpet ripped quickly away from under their feet, and posers and charlatans will be exposed faster than ever, thanks to a combination on the new social networking and the new financial system, which is wonderful news. I'm not, as I said previously, going to delve into the details of this change; however if you want to see the full extent of the causes and ramifications of this recession and the new way, I strongly suggest you read Ayn Rand's prophetic and very popular book, *Atlas Shrugged.*

Understand this: the new way will not be friendly toward entrepreneurs. That is why it is crucial that we are early adopters of the solution. In any crisis, quacks, con-artists, and fakes will quickly rise to the occasion to fleece naïve, desperate, and scared entrepreneurs, as with Y2K and the dotcom fiasco, preying ruthlessly on their panicked victims, so read this chapter carefully; it can make a huge difference to your future.

The solution to the new order (I am not a conspiracy theorist, just a practical old sod who understands what's going on and is street smart), the correct response, if you like, is the most sophisticated, practical, and effective business system ever devised. It is as old as money and business, yet only about 1% of the owners of small and medium-sized businesses understand and use it. It is based on the understanding of relationships, trust, value, leverage, and profit.

We are in business to make the maximum amount of net profit with the least amount of time, risk, and cost. Most small business owners are broke, self-employed salespeople who work too hard and too long, and risk far too much, for way too little. We are territorial, small-minded, egocentric, and afraid of our competition. We limit our income potential and put all our eggs in one basket. We're in for the quick buck, and that is abundantly clear when you watch the ridiculous pitch fest at any seminar or business networking event. We focus on sales and reputation instead of profit, and we spend a lot of time lying. North America is the capital of B.S.. Entrepreneurs have learned to dress mutton like lamb, and the thin veneer of success and wealth is easily scraped away by mature entrepreneurs. That has to change. Authenticity, relation-ships, reciprocity, integrity, and RESULTS will be the determining factors in the future. The B.S. simply won't fly anymore. The monkeys are already falling out of the trees – look around you.

What will we see? Many small businesses will fail – soon. Government business training will pick up momentum fast. That's like having a ravenous wolf babysit plump, young lambs. Many new restrictions, controls, taxes, and reporting requirements, spying systems, and financial controls will soon be implemented to "protect" us. The IRS and Revenue Canada will work more closely together, and your accountant, who is already a government spy (yes, he gets paid a commission on found money when he reports you to the government for questionable financial transactions) will get more power. But let's focus on the solution, instead of the problem, which will become more evident as you read.

"I'm free, and freedom tastes of reality. I told you what it's like to reach the highest high. You laughed, and said, 'Nothing's that simple'. But you've been told many times before, messiah pointed to the door, but no-one had the guts to leave the temple. I'm free!"
~ *The Who / Tommy.*

The Solution

The solution of which I speak has allowed me to retire twice: once in South Africa and then again in Canada after I immigrated here in December, 1997. It allows me to run my core business in one hour a day, with no overhead, cost, employees, licenses, leases, limitations, franchises, inventory, or selling. It is based on relationships, trust, integrity, results, value, reciprocation, and profit. Passive aggressive, politically correct posers don't like my kind of business (they HATE me), because they get exposed and I fire them from my organization. Our business is called DollarMakers because that is why we are in business, and it's what we do. We have an international, 22-year track record, and we have Members in 19 countries. We're good at what we do. (We should be, after all the mistakes we made over 22 years!) You should never take advice from anyone more screwed up than you are, and you should only learn from someone who already has what you want. We live our business philosophy.

This solution has been around forever, and yet, as I said, 99% of the owners of small and medium-sized businesses don't understand or use it. It is called Joint Ventures, or Strategic Alliances. I know that by the way they do business. I don't believe anything anyone tells me anymore – I have met too many liars and pretenders. I believe what they DO. Talk is cheap, and money buys the whiskey. Joint Ventures allow any business owner, in any industry or geographic location, (in fact, you don't even need a business or product or service in order to become a Joint Venture Broker) to double and quadruple their profits (note that I said PROFITS, not sales) with no cost, risk, or selling, and very little time.

DollarMakers is the world leader in training, supporting, and providing access to the owners of small and medium-sized business, individuals, and professionals. Our Membership spans 19 countries at the time of writing, and we have a proven track record. We fire Members who don't abide by our Code of Business Ethics, and all our business is based on Joint Ventures, so we walk our talk. What you see, is what you get.

Joint Ventures succeed when three things are in place, like the numbers on a combination lock:

1. Only JV with the right people. Relationship is everything. Don't partner with people who are hard up for money – desperate people do desperate things and justify their bad choices. I personally only JV with Members of DollarMakers and people who are referred to me. Your reputation is at stake when you associate with bad people, and you will be

judged by the company you keep. Anonymous Internet JV's are a thing of the past. People want to know who you are, touch you, talk with you, and have access to you. You can't hide behind your computer anymore.

Become A Money Magnet

2. Get the right training and support. DollarMakers provides all the training and support you need and it is very affordable, because we make money from our JV's, not from training and Membership fees. In fact, Membership in the DollarMakers Women's Club is free! Without sufficient or good training, you're like a truck driver trying to fly a 747.

3. Win/Win. Reciprocity. Everyone has to win. That way, you pay only for results, not promises. You can't get ripped off by so-called "Consultants" and "Coaches", and you avoid losing money on "Madvertising". On-going, generous

remuneration locks your JV partners in to long-term, wealth-building relationships.

If you have been in the army and been under fire (I have); if you have had to do business in a war-torn country with serious sanctions, currency restrictions, and immigration (I have – I ran a Holiday Inn in Rhodesia the year before the ruthless thug Mugabe became the president); and if you have immigrated to a new country, with a very different culture, and you didn't know anyone there (I did, nearly twelve years ago), then you know how important relationships are.

In the new world, relationships in business will be EVERYTHING.

By using leverage to access databases, resources, money, credit, time, reputation, perishable resources and hidden assets, and using contingency advertising and paying only for results, you remove the risk and increase your profits. Back end, JV income is always, all 100% profit. Sweet! Every resource you could possibly need is readily available through the magical medium of Joint Ventures.

Joint Ventures allow us to use trade and barter; to utilize systems to protect ourselves from predators; and to insulate our security. Multiple, residual income flows from a variety of industries, people, and geographic areas provides security; and the removal of risk allows one to be radically creative. Since little time is required to create a JV (or a DollarMaker, as we like to call Joint Ventures), you have no limit on the amount of money you can make, and it can happen FAST. It is by far the quickest, simplest way to climb out of a cash-flow problem. And your JV's can be high-tech, low-tech, slow-tech, or no-tech. There is simply no limit to what you can do.

"You can get anything you want out of life, if you're prepared to help enough other people to get what they want." ~ Zig Ziglar

Now, instead of mouthing off and prattling on about how wonderful Joint Ventures are, how they can solve your business and marketing problems, and how you can divest yourself of risk and time vampires, let me get specific. How can YOU use Joint Ventures RIGHT NOW in your business to increase sales and profits? At our Bootcamps and on our Online Bootcamp, we teach 29 proven, interchangeable systems. Our DollarMakers Certified Business Mentors have access to 49 systems that they can apply to six areas of your business. But we don't have place for that now, so I will focus on just ONE system here - one of many, but a good one!

Put Yourself In A Toll-Booth Position With JV's

"Come to the edge", he said. But they were afraid. "Come to the edge", he said.
They came, he pushed them, and they flew.

Do This And Make Money!

The DollarMakers Referral System

Fifteen Million Dollar Round Table insurance salesmen I trained at the Old Mutual Life Insurance Company in South Africa said that this was the best system they had ever learned. It is proven and effective, and will work in any setting, in any business, from a mortgage salesman to a dry cleaner, from a realtor to a flooring company, and from hardware stores to restaurants. And when you combine this with numerous other systems that we teach, you're unstoppable.

JV Brokers can also triangulate this system – use it between a seller and his referrer – but we won't discuss that lucrative option here.

This approach is **strategic, rather than tactical**, and that is why it works. JV Brokers are strategists: They see the Big Picture and they see business as a giant game, a kind of Monopoly game. If set up correctly, it works exceptionally well, and there is no risk or cost involved.

FIVE SIMPLE STEPS to Serious Success, a Profusion of Prospects, and a Bulging Bank Balance

ONE:

Every person you meet has a Hot Button. That is something they want really badly, or a problem they need solving – an urgent, all consuming need, a pet project (or a favourite pet), a vice, habit, or burning desire. The important thing is to shut up and listen long

135

enough to find out what it is. Ask open-ended questions. Delve down, dig deep, listen. You need to know what someone really, *really* wants (and perhaps needs) in order to make this system work. What keeps them awake at night? What are their secret desires? What are they embarrassed to tell you? What do they fear? What do they love?

It doesn't matter if the person is rich – everybody wants something, and often people feel they can't justify buying the thing they want. Guilt, relationships, embarrassment, priorities, all sorts of things can be barriers to people acquiring what they really want, whether they can easily afford to buy it themselves or not! A bald old oddball like myself who played the drums in a rock band as a kid and drives his wife nuts by drumming on everything in sight might secretly want a set of expensive electric drums that only he can hear on headphones, but he doesn't feel he can justify the luxury. (This isn't the case.) Someone may yearn for a holiday in an exotic place, or piano lessons, or a special fur coat, an introduction, recognition, membership in a top club, or a furry pet. Or a second car. Or a car for her offspring. Or pampering at a spa, or house cleaning or babysitting or a diamond ring – it matters not what they want. *But you need to know what that is.* Ask questions, find clues, do a bit of spy work, and you can find out what it is.

TWO:

1. What do you want to sell, that has a high profit margin or life-time net value? To whom do you want to sell that product or service? Or are you looking for a Center of Influence Joint Venture Partner (if you're in Network Marketing, this will apply to you too)? In other words, what do you want to sell, and to whom do you want to sell it?

2. In addition, what amount of commission are you prepared to pay (preferably on an on-going basis) per sale, or for the initial sale? It doesn't have to be money – you can trade all sorts of things, buy them that which they don't want to buy themselves, and reciprocate in many ways, depending on the Hot Button of the person you need to reward, but for the sake of this exercise, let's focus on money for this illustration.

3. And what is your closing ratio? In other words, if I referred ten qualified people to you, how many sales would you make, on average, conservatively?

THREE:

Once you know what their Hot Button is, approach people who can refer you to the prospects you want to sell to. You're offering them what they want (their Hot Button) in return for the referrals, so you have their undivided attention and commitment. I will give you an example of the approach later.

FOUR:

Set up and explain the SYSTEM. This is where you tell them exactly what they have to do in order for them to get what they want. Specifics and details are necessary. Tell them how it will work, and then get them to tell you what you have told them and what they understand. This ensures that you are both on the same page and that there are no misunderstandings. Put it in writing, too. (More information on this on the next pages).

FIVE:

Monitor and Manage the System. You can't delegate and then abdicate. You have to measure in order to manage and continually build the relationship. Regular, specific communication, with numbers and dates and times instead of vague generalities and fluff, is the mark or a true leader.

Right. Now let's go through an example of a good DollarMakers Referral System.

Fasten your seatbelt, put your seat in the upright position, and listen carefully, because this simple system can create more qualified prospects than you can handle!

After doing your homework and spending time with Gillian, you have established that what she wants more than anything else is to be able to buy her son a car to take himself to college and get around on his own. This will give her loads of free time to do what she really loves doing – raising turtles (Her Hot Button). Her passion is turtles, and she has pictures and ornaments of turtles all over her home, but raising turtles takes time, and she'd rather be doing that than behaving like an aging soccer mom and driving her gawky son Edmund all over the known world. On a scale of one to ten, she tells you her level of motivation to get transport for her offspring is on a par with her love for turtles – a *fifteen*. So you have her attention and commitment.

The reason why you approached Gillian is that her day job is calling on businesses that have bought office furniture from the company she works for. She sees at least six new businesses every day, and she has a great relationship with them. Your business is selling business insurance, and you would love to meet those business owners that Gillian is talking with.

NUMBERS:

- Your closing ratio is 3 or 4 out of ten. You sell three or four out of every ten referrals that you get.
- The average commission you are prepared to pay out per sale is $100.
- The cost of Edmund's car lease and insurance is around $400 per month, so the commission from four sales per month will pay for Edmund's automobile.
- Conservatively, working on a two out of ten closing ratio, you need twenty qualified referrals per month in order to make the four sales that will pay for Edmund's car. That's around five referrals per week.

APPROACH:

You call Gillian and arrange a business meeting. You tell her you have an exciting proposal for her that will make her turtles very happy.

At the meeting, you say, "Gillian, I know how badly you want to spend more time with your turtles and that you can accomplish this by buying young Edmund (undeserving as the little swine is, you think to yourself), a car. Well, I have a proposition for you. Now this may work for you, and it may not, *depending on how much you love your turtles*, but here it is. **I would like to buy Edmund a car.** Yes, I would like to pay for the lease and insurance, and you said that's around $400 per month, right? How do you feel about that?"

When she picks herself up off the floor, Gillian tells you she has suddenly fallen in love with you and wants to bear your child, even though you're a woman. She is eager to hear more, so you kindly accommodate her: "Gillian, this is how it is going to work. I close around two out of every ten qualified referrals I get. I pay $100 commission per sale, so I need a minimum of twenty referrals from you per month in order to make four sales, which will pay for Edmund's car lease and the insurance.

"You are calling on people who are ideal prospects for my business insurance product. Every time you leave a client's office (by *client* I mean the *owner* of the business, not a salesperson, a cleaner, or the Mother-in-Law), you do a Columbo-type turn, and say to him or her, **'By the way, Sheila, a very good friend of mine, Janet Long, is an expert in business insurance. She's professional, trustworthy, and has a great reputation. Here's her brochure. She offers a free, face-to-face, 30 minute consultation to show you how to protect yourself from lawsuits and all sorts of dangerous situations at very little cost. There's no obligation or pressure, and she has saved many of my friends a lot of money. Please read this brochure. <u>May I ask her to call you?</u>'**

"That's all you say. Don't answer questions; just ask for permission to have me call them. If they say, 'Yes, by all means', add their name, particulars, and any other details that might help me (we can discuss this later) to make the sale to your referral list.

"You see about six new people a day, and I need a minimum of five referrals per week, so shoot for six or seven (or more) referrals per week, but at least five. These are people who have given you permission to have me call them, and they have my brochure. If only 20% of them agree to have me call them, you will be sending me six referrals every Friday afternoon or evening, before 6pm, by e-mail. I need their name, address, telephone and e-mail address, and any details you think might help me make a good connection with them. I will be professional, not pushy, and I assure you I would not hard sell or upset any of your customers. If I make more sales, you get more money, so after paying for Edmund's wheels, you can use the extra money to buy that new Turtle Palace you want so badly. What do you think?"

If Gillian agrees to this, spend some time explaining your business to her and motivating her, practice and role-play the script, and make sure she understands exactly how this is all going to work, and that she is accountable to send you the referrals every Friday, and then accompany her to the dealership to buy the car. You now have her locked in to sending you at least five qualified referrals every week. Naturally, you need to communicate with her regularly to motivate and encourage her, and get her back on track if she slackens or is late with her referrals.

Do this with TEN people, so you now have FIFTY qualified referrals per week. If you have salespeople, teach each of them to develop ten referral centers. What will that do for your sales and your bottom line?

As a broker, you could set up these systems for other businesses, and earn a piece of all the ongoing commissions.

You're paying for results, not promises, so you can scrap your expensive and risky advertising when this lucrative system starts working for you.

Some people can send you more referrals than others, some will be able to email their entire database with your offers of free reports, conference calls, seminars, or CD's. You can have people give away gift certificates for free samples of your products or services – I could go on all day, and elaborate on possibilities all night, but this simple referral system works beautifully if properly set up and managed. In many cases, buying people things or trading things is much cheaper than paying them money.

Turn every happy customer and every Center of Influence into a Paid Referral Center for your business.

This system demonstrates the Joint Venture Mindset: It's not about you, and you can leverage other peoples' resources in a win/win scenario. Remove risk, boost your profits through the roof, add value, and blow your competition out of the water.

If you have any questions, and for more information, free e-book downloads, training, videos, Membership options, access to our Mentors, articles, podcasts, and more, visit our website: **www.DollarMakers.com**, or email me with your specific questions to robin@dollarMakers.com

Now Go Forth and Joint Venture!

Robin J. Elliott started his business in 1987 and is an internationally recognized entrepreneur, trainer, and speaker. He is the author of eleven books. His company, Elliott Enterprises Inc., trading as <u>DollarMakers.com</u>, is the world leader in Joint Venture training, support, and access for small and medium-sized businesses, professionals, and individual entrepreneurs with

 Members in twenty different countries. He regularly presents seminars and *Joint Venture Broker Bootcamps* across North America and the United Kingdom.

He is known for his no B.S., politically incorrect, fearless straight talk and love of "laissez faire" capitalism. His favourite saying is, *"talk is cheap, but money buys the whiskey"*, and his favourite book is *Atlas Shrugged* by Ayn Rand. Mr. Elliott immigrated with his wife, successful entrepreneur Rika Elliott, from South Africa to Canada December 1st, 1997. They live happily in Vancouver, in beautiful British Columbia. The mission of DollarMakers is to help people around the world achieve financial freedom through the use of Joint Ventures.

FREE Gift Offer! Get over $595.00 in additional marketing and business building special reports, audio CD's and DVD's mailed right to your door. See page 271 for complete details, or visit: **www.ResultsEnterprises.com/gift.html**

Notes & Thoughts!

THE 3 BIGGEST MARKETING SINS AND HOW TO AVOID THEM

By Dave Dubeau

Most Canadian small business owners, entrepreneurs, and professionals are very competent at delivering their core product or service.

Unfortunately, most of them are not competent at getting the word out about their product or service through effective and trackable marketing. They are depriving themselves, their families, and their employees of profits they could and should be enjoying because they are committing Marketing "sins" in their businesses.

Here are the 3 biggest Marketing "sins" that, once you repent and mend your ways about, will help pave your way to the holy land of increased profits!

SIN # 1: Thou Shalt Not Be a Marketing "Casanova"; Instead, Thou Shalt Become a "Sheik" with a Harem"

Now please don't get all offended (or excited) by the title of this topic – about not being a "Marketing Casanova" and instead having a "harem". I don't want you to think that I am a completely sexist, male chauvinist pig (yet). I am simply using this as a memorable analogy about focusing exclusively on getting new clients, patients, and customers as opposed to maximizing the value of the ones you have already.

As we show elsewhere in this book, there are only three ways to grow ANY business:

- **Increase the Average Transaction Value.** (Get them to spend more)
- **Increase the Frequency of Purchase.** (Get them to buy more often)
- **Increase the Number of Customers.** (Get more of them in the door).

Unfortunately, almost everyone focuses exclusively on the last tactic, getting more "new" customers. Although important, it is very costly and very time consuming. You have probably heard the old statistic that it costs 5 to 7 times more to get a new customer to buy from you than it does to get a current or past customer to buy from you again. It may be a well-worn stat, but it is very true.

That is why I use the "Casanova" and "Harem" analogy. The life of a "Casanova" might seem exciting – being a "stud" and picking up a different lover (customer) whenever he wants to (or at least trying to…I don't think that even Casanova got lucky that often)!

However, the whole process of seduction (in our case, attracting a new customer) is very time, energy, and money consuming. You have to get their attention (advertise, market), make yourself as attractive to them as possible (Unique Selling Proposition), shower them with attention and gifts (discounts, bonuses, offers), convince them that you are the right choice for them (guarantees, warranties, testimonials etc.) and then consummate the relationship (make the sale).

A Marketing Casanova – Where's The Next Conquest?

A Casanova then completely forgets the lover (customer) he just seduced (acquired) and immediately chases after another new one, starting the whole process over again (and probably angering his last "conquest" by his lack of on-going affection). Wham-Bam, Thank-you Ma'am.

Now hopefully your customers do not react or feel as strongly as a shunted lover, but they do subconsciously resent not being appreciated more after the initial sale.

Now what if our "Casanova" had a different mindset and turned himself into a "Sheik" with a harem?

As a Marketing "Sheik" he would initially work hard at attracting his "wives" (customers) to him, just as Casanova does with his "lovers". But then, instead of forgetting about them after the initial dalliance (sale), he would bring them into his harem, to be his forever more.

Once the new wife is a part of his harem, our sheik now has the opportunity to consummate the relationship as often as he likes (repeat sales). Instead of just one lover at a time, he has many "wives" he can choose from. And if he wishes, he can have a wife (customer) every single night (instead of just sporadically like our slutty friend Casanova).

A Happy Marketing Sheik With His Harem

Now, being a good sheik, having a harem back home wouldn't stop him from looking for more wives (customers) to add to it – but it wouldn't have to be the entire focus of his life. And while he pursues a new one he would be much more relaxed and at ease about it as his needs are more than covered already by all of the current wives he has in the harem.

Looking at this example with fresh eyes, it does sound pretty sexist... so sue me! It's still a helluva good analogy.

Let's observe this from a business perspective. Look at your own situation. When you have plenty of business happening, you are relaxed and at ease when dealing with new customers and prospects. You are polite and accommodating – and definitely not desperate. If they do business with you, great. If not, it's no big deal because you've got a lot of customers already.

This is a much more pleasant business situation to be in!

As Steve Chandler, a mentor of mine likes to say, *"Needy is Creepy"*. Most of us don't like to deal with "needy" people – they give off the wrong, desperate vibe.

This brings to mind an experience I had lately...

I was in a Vancouver mall awhile back, killing time while my wife was shopping (I had a lot of time to kill...my wife is an accomplished shopper, and coming from our small town of Kamloops, "big city" malls are her favourite places). I wandered into one of those art galleries where they sell prints, do framing, etc. There was a handwritten sign up saying "today, everything 40% off".

The store was empty, and the store owner looked at me the way I imagine a hungry lion would look at a fat, juicy, and slow-moving wildebeest!

When I walked in, he jumped up from behind the counter and came rushing out. There was a perfunctory "hello", and then his eyes were glued to me as I wandered around. I could feel him watching me, his gaze seemed to be directed at my derriere. (Being a 'red-neck" from Fort St. John originally, I wasn't sure if I should feel flattered or offended!) Then I realized that his eyes were locked on my wallet and not my "ass..ets".

Either way, it was a creepy sensation. I was just looking at different pictures, and he scooted up beside me asking, "Is there anything that interests you? What do you like? I can get it for you?" And then the ultimate desperation clincher, "I can even give you a better deal than the 40% off if you want." The look in his eyes implored, "Please buy something from me... anything! Please, please, please!"

Talk about "needy" (and creepy). Now don't get me wrong. I felt sorry for the guy. Business was slow, and his rent was probably due that day or the next, and he was obviously feeling the money squeeze.

But feeling sorry for him doesn't mean I'm going to buy some piece of art I didn't even want. I was not a good prospect for him – I wasn't interested in anything – and even if I were slightly interested in buying something, he creeped me out so much, I just wanted to get out of there FAST. His desperation repelled me. And I'm sure he had the same effect on a lot of people.

That got me thinking about the difference between his art gallery, and the one my clients Mark and Lila Phillips have in Sherwood Park, Alberta. Same kind of business, in a mall, but very different results. You see, they have been collecting their customer's contact information for years, and they now have a database of close to 15,000 people! When they want a sales–surge, they contact those folks and get them to come in to buy from them again. And again... And again. They don't have to resort to handwritten "40% off today" signs, or pitiful, desperate begging for business. That helps to explain why they have a 20+ year business that continues to grow, and this guy probably won't be around the next time I'm in that mall. He was a marketing "Casanova", while Mark and Lila have a strong "Harem" of customers.

Bottom line is, this is why you need to spend time on getting people to spend more with you, and to purchase more often instead of just chasing after new ones all the time.

CURES FOR SIN # 1

OK, by now you hopefully agree with me that just focusing your marketing on getting new customers and being a Marketing Casanova is bad, and that creating a Harem of customers to sell more to, more often, is good.

So here are some nuts and bolts strategies you can use to do it:

1. Make sure you have a Good Customer Database

It's always amazing to me that more business owners don't keep track of who their customers are. If this is you, don't feel too bad because you have a lot of company. However, being one of the "blind following the blind" is nothing to be proud of either – so let's get you shaped up, shall we?

And if you do already have a good, clean, customer database – good for you! However, if you have it, but haven't been using it, then not-so-good.

So the first thing to do is to make the decision that you are going to put as many of your customers/ clients/ patients into a database as possible.

Now this is easier for some businesses than others. Doctors, lawyers, financial planners, insurance people, etc. tend to have all of their customers'/ clients'/ patients' data on file, because that is part of the process of doing business with them.

But what about a restaurant, brick and mortar store, etc.? What about those businesses where the customers don't have to provide their contact information? How do we get it from them?

Well, I suggest you DON'T do what Radio Shack used to do – make it obligatory when you bought something. Instead, you should figure out ways to make them WANT to give their contact information to you. I find that "ethical bribes" work well. Here are four proven ways to do it:

- Have a draw for free products/ services/ trips, etc.
- Create a "Club" with valuable benefits for membership.
- Offer to mail them a free gift or discount coupon in the mail (and another one by e-mail – that way you get their physical and their e-mail address).

♦ Simply ask them for it, so that you can let them know what is happening with your business. Add them to your newsletter list, etc.

OK, now that you are quickly building up your company database, comes the part that will get you RESULTS...

2. Communicate more and more often with current and past customers. Way more often.

It's not good enough to just have a client/ customer/ patient database unless you actually do something with it!

The marketing purpose of having this database is so that you can communicate with your customers on a regular basis.

How regular you ask? Well, there are different opinions about this, but I would say at LEAST once a month. If you really want to rock and roll, then you want to do it once a week. And if that sounds like a lot to you, consider this: I know of a gentleman who "touches" his database one to two times... a DAY!

Now that is a little excessive if you ask me, but it works for him (he is a very sharp marketer, with a multi-million dollar a year business).

Personally, I think that most business owners would do well to send out one mail piece per month to their dbase, and one e-mail per week. That makes a total of 64 "touches" a year (give or take).

Important note: You want to make sure that not all of these "touches" are sales-focused; that is too much.

64 touches sound tough for you? It really isn't. In fact, you can pretty much do it automatically with very little work on your part.

For the monthly mailings – you can create a printed **monthly newsletter** to send everyone.

Keep it fun and light. Include a lot of personality about you and your staff. Include fun cartoons, recipes, etc. that aren't necessarily related to your business. Do a couple of articles that are related to what you do. The idea is to build up a relationship over time with your customers. They should start to look forward to getting your newsletter, and miss it if they don't! (You know you are doing a really good job when you get complaint calls that someone did NOT get their regular monthly newsletter from you – or when people voluntarily give you their new address when they move so they won't miss any of them).

Creating and producing a monthly printed newsletter is intimidating for a lot of people, so a great "done for you" resource is **www.readytogonewsletters.com**. This company provides some really good general interest newsletter templates for both business to business (B2B) or business to consumer (B2C) markets, as well as some industry specific options (realtors, insurance agents, financial planners, etc). All you have to do is get the template, add your name, contact info, and photo (if you want) and voila! Your newsletter is done! Of course, if you want to modify it and add more personalized content, you can do that too (and I suggest you do).

You then either print out the documents yourself on your office photocopier or send them to your printer and have them do it.

These monthly newsletters also are a great place to promote your featured products or services – as well as provide information about special events or sales.

On top of that, you can include greeting cards for special occasions and holidays, Christmas, Valentine's Day, birthdays, anniversaries, etc. That can be another easy 8 – 12 direct "touches" if you want.

A good option for doing this automatically is through **www.sendoutcards.com**. They offer ready-to-go greeting cards, birthday cards, and holiday cards you can set up to go out to one person or thousands of people at a time. The best thing about it is that it is automatic! You set it up, and their system does all of the rest: prints the cards, puts in your message (even in your own handwriting if you want!), personalizes it, puts it in an envelope, stamps it, and sends it for you! Doesn't get much easier than that!

For weekly e-mails you can offer a weekly tip about your area of expertise, a joke of the week, etc. Then from time to time you can promote something as well.

Occasionally you may even want to give them a phone call to see how things are going, do a survey, or invite them to a "client appreciation" event. (Many people are scared of this due to the "do-not-call" lists. However, if they have done business with you recently you should be OK. But I'm not a lawyer and I can't give legal advice, so check out the complete information about this at **https://www.lnnte-dncl.gc.ca/index-eng**). If you can do it, I highly recommend phone contact. Done properly, it is very powerful and very effective.

Again, keep in mind the BIG goal – to keep YOU in your customers' minds. You want to nurture your relationship with them. You want to be the "obvious choice" when they think of your business category. You want to keep your communications light and personal – not stiff and formal (think "letter from Aunt Marge" vs. "letter from my bank"). You want to focus on more than just selling as well, so not all of your communication is "salesy".

3. Keep it Fresh with NEW & Improved, Events, "widgets", etc.

Have you ever wondered why it seems that such mundane things like laundry detergent, dishwashing soap, shampoo, and paper towels always seem to be getting modified and changed? New and Improved ACME detergent, with ultra-white bleach pellets! New and Improved SNOTTIES facial tissue with aloe vera infused comfort pouches, and so on. It never ends! How many ways can you improve this kind of stuff? Lots, evidently.

Big companies like Proctor & Gamble and Kimberly Clark know that their customers always like something "new & improved" and it spices up an otherwise completely boring product! Not only that, but it helps to keep their customers loyal, and not be seduced by the competition.

You should look at how you can do that in your business as well.

One of the best ways is to introduce a really high-priced version of what you do/ sell.

So, for example, if your regular product/ service "A" costs $100.00 with a profit margin of $50.00, then you create "Whizbang product/ service B" with a bunch of extras and improvements, and you charge $397.00 for it (with a profit margin of $250.00).

This accomplishes a few things:

1. It may provide you with some very high ticket sales, with fantastic profit margins. In any customer base, there are some people who simply want the very best and are willing to pay top dollar for it. Why not offer that, and take advantage of that pent up demand? If you don't do it, chances are they will be lured away by a competitor who does.

2. Even if you don't sell a single one of the "high-priced" options, just having that as a point of comparison with your "normal" price will make the latter seem like a real bargain.

You can also try doing different versions of what you have. If it's already very high-priced, you could try offering a stripped down version for a lower cost (but still with a profit margin that makes it worthwhile for you).

Offer different varieties for different needs/ tastes etc.

Bundle different products/ services together to create packages.

You get the idea.

The bottom line is, the more variety you give your customers, the more reasons you have to contact them, and the more you will keep their interest.

Rolling out something "New" on a regular basis helps you to do that.

Now, speaking of keeping their interest, that brings us to the second of our Marketing Sins:

SIN # 2: Thy Marketing Shall Not Be BORING!

It's a real toss-up between which sin is worse: being a Casanova or being BORING. Both are bad! Really bad!

Yawn... What BORING Marketing!

Nowadays, we are all bombarded by a phenomenal amount of advertising and marketing. Consciously and subconsciously we are all exposed to literally thousands of advertising impressions every day (think: print ads in newspapers, magazines, billboards, commercials on TV, radio, internet, our cell phones, promo products around your office/ home, bus stop signs, flyers, direct mail, signage on and in stores, on cars, and even in public bathrooms! It never ends!).

Think about it for a minute – our grandparents or great grandparents growing up on the farm were only exposed to about 1% of the marketing that we and our customers and prospective customers are exposed to!

That is the kind of competition your marketing and advertising is up against to get attention. So DON'T BE BORING!

I think many, if not most, business owners completely underestimate the challenge of getting a prospect's attention. This, combined with the fact that most advertising sales people do not have the faintest clue about what kind of advertisements actually work, helps feed the bland and boring scene that most advertising falls into.

Then, to top it all off, most advertising sales reps will baffle and confound their advertisers with advice about "branding" and the need for a lot of "repetition". They will try to convince you that your ad should be "pretty", be a soft sell, and have lots of "white" space for aesthetics.

Their main goal is to create as much revenue FROM you as possible, and to keep it coming for as long as possible. They encourage you to have ads that are hard or impossible, to track – and baffle you with bullshit about "branding" your company and getting your name out there. This way they don't have any real accountability for how effective (or, more likely, ineffective) the ad is.

(That's why we all, in this book, talk so much about only using trackable and accountable marketing – and that is direct response marketing).

And then another big reason for boring advertising is because so many advertisers are WIMPS and MAMA's BOYS (and GIRLS).

Canada is such a friendly and accommodating country. We are very polite and gentle. Generally speaking, everyone has a pleasant or at least neutral feeling about us. We try hard to be "liked" and modest, and of course, we always try to be sensitive to others and politically correct.

It's kind of like vanilla ice cream: nice and BLAND.

That might be OK for diplomacy and international relations, but it absolutely SUCKS for your marketing.

There is, however, another uniquely Canadian activity that exemplifies what your marketing should be like: Hockey!

I think we need to look more at HOCKEY as an example of what to do when it comes to Canadian Marketing. I don't see any "meekness" or "timidness" in hockey. I see aggressive, in-your-face, up against the boards, drop-the-gloves-and-go-at-'er adrenaline-pumping ACTION!! Hockey is definitely NOT boring – and your marketing shouldn't be either.

Marketing guru, and my long-distance mentor, Dan Kennedy, says, "You have to repel to attract".

Most of us loathe to offend anyone for fear of what they might say about us, or think about us. We hold out the unrealistic hope that everyone is a potential customer, or may become one.

The fact is, the tighter you define exactly who your ideal customer/ client/ prospect is, the better. And just about as important as that is to define exactly who you DON'T want to attract as a customer.

And then there is the issue that really amuses me: business owners and professionals worrying about what other people in their industry will think or say about them if they rock the boat with their marketing.

That one is really a classic.

This is basically worrying about what your competition thinks of you! WHO THE HELL CARES??

They aren't looking out for your back. It's survival of the fittest out there, and you have to look out for yourself. If your business or practice were to go down the tube tomorrow, most of your competitors would jump for joy and wonder how many of your customers they would get.

You don't see a hockey team worried about scoring too many goals against the rival team, do you? If they are ahead in the game, they don't slow down to let the opposing team catch up, so that it will be a more enjoyable game for them and their fans. If they can win the game 12 – 0, that's GREAT!

Now I'm not saying that your overriding goal in business is to screw it to your competitors, because it isn't. Your overriding goal in business should be to serve as many customers as you can (or want) and, in doing so, create an exceptional profit for your efforts.

If doing that involves ticking off your competition, or bucking the norms of your industry, then so be it. It's your business, and your life. They don't give a crap about you, so don't worry yourself about them and what they say.

Solutions to Boring Advertising...

First of all it is important to understand that **not every breathing body is a good prospect for your business.**

So take a few moments to visualize your ideal customer right now. Think back about who your best customers in the past and currently have been. Get as much detail as you can about them. Remember everything you can about them: Male or female. Married or single. Age. Occupation. How much money they make. Where they live. What they drive. Where they eat. What they do for recreation. What do they read? What shows do they watch? What is their political affiliation? Religion? etc.

Once you have that "ideal" customer planted firmly in your mind, then the goal is to attract as many more like them as possible.

Another marketing mentor of mine, Bill Glazer, suggests that you create a mental picture of that person in your mind, and then give that picture a name (for example, Fred).

Then, all of your marketing messages should be directed right at THEM, and only them. Create it as if you are talking directly to your "Fred".

Then go and do the same exercise with your worst customers. Create an image in your mind of what they are like.

Then part of your marketing messages should focus on repelling THEM.

This follows Kennedy's motto to "repel to attract". You should almost be creating an "us against them" sensation.

On the following page is an example of some copy I used in one of the sales letters to promote a Real Estate training event with our Fast Track to Cash Flow group of people.

As you can see, I very clearly define the kind of person I want to come out, as well as the person I do not want. Does this offend some people? Sure it does. But the people it offends (repels) are NOT my customers, and probably never will be. So it doesn't matter to me, because I am attracting exactly the right people to me instead.

You'll notice that I left in some of the copy enhancements in the letter (they might not be "pretty", but they sure do grab attention and get results) and cannot be accused of being boring!

But is it right for me? Can I actually do this stuff?

Sourpuss Sam: "I have to give you credit Darren, this event does sound very impressive. But is it really for me? I mean, can just anybody come and immediately become a success at this?"

I'm glad you asked Sam. The **'09 FTIC Real Estate 2 Day Intensive Workshop** is definitely NOT for everyone. Let's take a look at...

"Sour-Puss Sam"

Who Should Attend

- Anyone who is looking for a fun way to make lot's of money without having to spend years of work and *many* thousands of dollars to "figure it out" themselves.
- Employees who are sick and tired of seeing all of their efforts pay off BIG for their employer, but not for themselves.
- Anyone who has thought about getting into Real Estate, but who hasn't taken the leap yet.
- Professionals seeking a new career or a part-time supplement.
- Anyone who wants to build a passive income stream and retire in a few short years.
- Anyone who has purchased the original "Fast Track to Real Estate" course and wants to get the newest enhancements to the course fast, get trained personally by Darren and his advisors, and meet other serious investors.

Who Should NOT Attend

- Snivelers, wimps, whiners, couch potatoes, and anyone else who thinks the world owes them a living and are a pain in the butt to be around.
- Anyone who thinks we can wave a magic wand and make you rich and that it doesn't involve work. Sorry, Real Estate investing is a true business and comes with the same requirements it takes to get rich just like in any business. Real Estate is the vehicle...you provide the fuel.
- Anyone so void of GUTS that they'll let their broke friends and relatives kill their dreams and talk them out of attending.

I'm sorry to be so brutally blunt, but this is a unique event for a small audience. I only want the BEST people to come. This doesn't mean you have to be a "super(wo)man", or a genius. It just means that I want to work with people who have the right attitude. Folks who are open-minded, and willing to act on what they learn.

And if you like what you have read in this letter so far, you are most probably exactly the kind of person who will benefit most from this unique event.

Let's Quickly Summarize, Because......

We're packing so much into this 2009 FTIC Real Estate 2 Day Intensive Workshop, you've already forgot some of it from earlier pages!

When you register for this incredible week-end event, you'll get the following:

I. The LIVE 2009 FTIC Real Estate 2 Intensive Workshop! Limited to only 97 Attendees (some of whom may bring a guest).

What should this accomplish for you?

Done properly, you will attract a lot more of the exact client you are looking for – and the ones you enjoy working with. That means more profits, and more enjoyment at work. That's what it's all about isn't it?

Will you offend some people? Of course you will! Especially the ones you don't want to work with! You may get indignant letters or calls from time to time from one of these twits… SO WHAT?? You don't want or need them.

Think about it from a hockey perspective again. Successful teams focus on pleasing their hometown fans. That is their main goal – why? Because those are the people who pay the bills (and their incredibly high salaries). The more they antagonize the opposing team's fans, the better! That builds up even more loyalty and fanaticism from their own followers. The same will hold true for you and your customers.

Now go and Create a Great U.S.P. & Guarantee(s)

Having generic tag-lines, mission statements, and guarantees is BORING. You need to stand out with these as well – and really give your prospective customers strong reasons to work with you.

Let's go with the old classic tag line first. Many business owners work hard (or not) to create their logos and tag lines, coming up with such scintillating classics like (taken from my local Yellow Pages book):

"Operating & Serving the ... area since 1974" (Brake shop) – So What? Is that going to suck me in like a Hoover vacuum in overdrive? I don't think so.

"Products and Services from the Company You Trust" (Furnace sales & repairs). Oooh, I'm feeling faint from all the excitement.

"Best Pizza & Ribs in Town" (Pizza joint). Wow! That is believable and exciting...NOT.

OK, it is easy enough to bash these guys about their boring tag lines, but what is an example of a good one?

Well, probably the most famous tag-line (or, as we like to call them, U.S.P. – Unique Selling Proposition) is the old one from Domino's Pizza "Fresh, hot pizza delivered to your door in 30 minutes or less...Guaranteed".

That is probably as close to a perfect U.S.P. as you can get. It gets the major points across quickly and clearly. Fresh & Hot pizza. Fast. Guaranteed.

It helped take them from a broke college drop-out's start up company to becoming the leader in their very competitive market within 10 years.

From my previous life as an English Language School owner, training employees on-site for corporate clients like Cisco Systems, Dole Fruit Company, Kimberly Clark and Bayer pharmaceuticals in Costa Rica, my U.S.P. was "We'll create your program for you, provide all of the materials, and you can try our classes for a full month. If you aren't thrilled for any reason, you pay nothing, and you keep the materials".

This was a pretty "ballsy" offer, because that often involved me going out on the limb for thousands of dollars in material costs, course preparations, and teachers' salaries. The client only paid AFTER the fact – and only if they were satisfied.

However, kind of like the Domino's example, this helped take my company from a start-up to being in the top 3 in the country (out of over 50 direct and indirect competitors) within 2.5 years.

When I had time and was working as a freelance marketing consultant in Canada, my USP/ Guarantee was this:

"If, after our consultation, you don't think the tactics and strategies I have given you will create at least $15,000.00 in profits you wouldn't have had otherwise, the consultation is FREE, and I'll pay you $200.00 Cash for wasting your time".

You'll notice that these examples include a guarantee about the product or service – and that is what makes them so powerful. This is what marketing guru Jay Abraham refers to as "Risk Reversal": You take all of the risk away from the client and put it right on your own shoulders.

That brings up the topic of Guarantees

If you don't have one, you should – and FAST. The reality is that you probably have one anyway, but you just don't promote it well.

If a client were truly unsatisfied with your product or service, let you know about it, and threatened to call the Better Business Bureau, the press, and your mother-in-law to tell them all about it, would you give them their money back? Yes, you probably would. If that is the case, then you do guarantee your stuff! You just don't like the idea of advertising the fact!

Time to change your mind.

By offering a good, solid guarantee, you are creating risk reversal, and taking away one of the blocks that people have about doing business with you – being worried that they are going to get ripped off.

With a good guarantee (or even better, multiple guarantees) you will attract more customers and you can charge higher prices. Period.

And will you get taken up on your guarantee from time to time? Will you get ripped off by unscrupulous customers from time to time?

Yep. So what? Once you get over the "ego-hit" from it, just consider it to be a cost of doing business. Because, done right, having a good guarantee will attract far more business and profits to you than money you will ever pay out in living up to the guarantee.

And if you find that you are getting a lot of people requesting their money back, then you are either providing a product or service that is below average (in which case fix it, or start offering a different product/ service), or you are dealing with a very cheap and sleazy market (and in that case, you are attracting the wrong people – fix your message and attract the right ones).

People often ask me if I ever had to live up to my guarantees in my language school business. In the 14 years we had it, we were taken up on it twice. In both cases it was because we dropped the ball with our service (the teachers were not up to par) and the client was justified in getting their money back. Never once did we get ripped off.

With Fast Track to Cash Flow, we always offer phenomenal guarantees with our events. Typically, it is a "Money-Back-Plus-a-Penalty" kind of thing, where we will refund them their entire investment PLUS give them between $100 and $800 (depending on how much the event price was) cash.

In the 3 years we've been doing this, we've been taken up on that guarantee a handful of times. Sometimes it was from a legitimate complaint, and a few times we were "ripped-off". But when we look at the overall effect of having the guarantee in increased numbers of people attending, and in gross revenues, we are more than happy to do it. It makes GREAT economic sense.

So take a good hard look at your own business. Define exactly who your ideal customer is (and who you want to repel). Come up with something that really differentiates you from your competition (a good U.S.P.) and see how you can integrate guarantees into your business.

Doing this will help you focus on attracting more of exactly the kind of customers you are looking for, and making you the obvious choice for them.

Does this require some effort and time on your part? Of course it does. Nothing worthwhile is a cake-walk, and that brings up our 3rd and final sin:

SIN # 3: Thou Shall Not Be a Lazy Marketer

Laziness in Marketing is relying on only one or two marketing media to attract new customers.

Now, at the outset this might seem to be a logical thing to do. Once you find the marketing media that works best for you, then you keep using it and you don't worry about anything else.

So, for example, before I began working with Darren Weeks and Fast Track to Cash Flow, marketing his "How to Get Rich in Canada" events, they had focused exclusively on advertising the events in the newspapers.

Lazy Marketers Lose... Sooner Or Later!

Now that I am in charge, we still do newspaper advertising (which is still our # 1 way to attract people), but we have also started using postcards (our # 2 method), radio, TV, posters, TV channel listings, infomercials, tradeshows, billboards, doorknob ads, publicity, social media (Facebook), flyers, mobile billboards, and more.

Now I am the first to admit that not all of it works well, and nothing comes close to the newspapers which bring in about 55% of the total. But as long as the cost per lead fits within our parameters, it makes sense to keep doing it. By adding on these other media, we are reaching the 45% we would have missed by doing newspapers alone.

"Marketing Diversity Leads to Stability" – Bill Glazer.

Most small business owners only do one or two forms of advertising. Quite often it isn't even because it works that well (because they don't know how to track it), but because the ad sales person did a good job selling them the advertising.

And if you do track your results and know that the advertising is working, I still suggest you test different media, and get as many different ones working for you as possible.

This is for several reasons:

1. It will help you to grow your business faster and make more money! That is the obvious one! If you are using two different advertising media and getting 100 new customers, then if you add 4 or 5 more media and only get 25 more customers, you have still increased your business by 25%!

2. You never know when your best advertising media will disappear! I know this sounds a little paranoid, but this is a very real concern. "Cold" Telemarketing has been eliminated for a lot of businesses. "Cold" Fax marketing was made illegal in the USA. The mail doesn't work when the postal workers are on strike. Infomercials were illegal on TV for a few years. Newspapers are cutting back staff and expenses, and some of them might go under. It goes on and on. If you are dependant on only one or two sources of customers, and it is taken away from you suddenly, then you are screwed.

3. Advertising in different media helps to grow the "whole". If you are only in one or two places, you are easy to miss. If you are advertising in 5, 6, or 12 different ways, you become omnipresent and appear to be very strong and stable. People might respond to one type of marketing, but your other marketing they have seen or heard of helps to confirm their decision. This is the only "branding" you should be trying to get – having all of your direct response advertising feed each other and grow the whole.

You Must Create a Marketing Parthenon.

So if you are reliant upon only a few different ways of marketing and advertising, you need to start branching out and trying new and different media.

For example, if you've only ever advertised in the Yellow Pages, start experimenting with direct mail.

If you've always been an "offline" person, start doing some on-line advertising.

If you've only done radio, try some print and TV.

The key here is to TRACK everything that you do. How? It's pretty easy. Make sure there is a call to action in all advertising you do (see Shane Morgan's chapter for more about that). Use a different tracking mechanism for each ad you do. This could be a different promotion code, a different phone number they call, a different person they ask for on the phone, a different website they visit (see Sam Beckford's chapter for examples of that), or a different bonus or discount they request etc.

You track how much the advertising cost you, how many leads it got you, and how many sales you got from it. If it is productive, keep doing it.

This brings up the next question:

What is "Productive" Marketing?

Short answer: any marketing that makes economic sense to do.

For most of us, that means that if we have a product or service that is NOT a one-shot wonder, and there is a good chance that the new customer will do business with us again in the future, then we should be satisfied if we break even on the advertising.

For example: We spend $1,000.00 on the advertising. At the end of the promotion we calculate that we created $3,000.00 worth of sales, with a net profit of $1,112.00.

Net profit minus Cost of advertising ($1,112 – 1,000 = $112). In that case, I would consider the marketing to be successful. Why? Because it will be a lot less expensive (or even free) to get those people to come back again to buy from us. And then the profit margin will be practically pure profit without much marketing expense.

Now this is a difficult concept for most people to understand. They think, "If I spend $1,000 on marketing, it should get me $5,000, $10,000 or even $20,000 in pure PROFIT right away!" But that is completely short-sighted and unrealistic. It does happen from time to time, but if it always worked that way, we'd all be mega millionaires already!

In fact, some businesses do very well by going NEGATIVE to attract a new customer.

At Fast Track to Cash Flow we invest (notice I use that word, not "spend") between $30,000 and $100,000 to advertise for our FREE events! It costs us, on average, $100.00 to get a person out to one of our free introductory events. We don't even pitch the people anything once they get to the event! They can buy a book, or take a $10 "test-drive" of our membership program, but there is no pressure for them to do so. Our sales of these things don't even make a dent in our marketing investment.

That is because our initial goal is to start a relationship with the person. We give education to do that, and it builds up our credibility in the eye of the attendee.

We then invite them out to other free events focused on specific investment and other opportunities. If they like what they hear and see there, then they may choose to invest with us, and that is when we generate revenue.

I've heard indirectly from Dan Kennedy that the billion dollar Guthy Renker company that sells the acne treatment on TV (name: Renu) actually goes negative for 5 months with every new customer they get. That means that they have to sell them their monthly batch of zit goop for 6 full months to see any profit! However, the model works for them, and they have the bank account to show for it.

Guthy Renker goes negative for 5 months; we "invest" over $100.00 to get a person out to a FREE "no-pitch" event. Guthy Renker is a billion dollar company, and Fast Track has grown ten fold in the last three years.

That's because both companies understand **The Lifetime Value of a Customer (LTV)**.

This is probably the MOST important number you can figure out for your business, as it will give you a benchmark upon which to decide if your marketing is paying for itself or not.

I'll use the example I am most familiar with from my 10 + years of owning and running my corporate language training company in Costa Rica. Typically we worked with small group classes.

Average charge per group/per month: $500.00
Average # of groups per client: 2.5
Average length of relationship: 21 months.

So the gross revenues were: $500 x 2.5 x 21 = $26,250.00

Our "hard" costs for delivering the service were 45%, so that left 55% gross profit (before office overhead).

$26,250 x .55 = $14,437.50

So that meant to me that every NEW client meant on average, $14,400 to my business over a 21 month period.

This made the gross lifetime value of a client $26,250.00, and
The gross net lifetime value of a client $14,437.50.

(If you took into account that on average, every client referred .5 NEW clients who increases that value by another $13K gross, and $7K gross net.)

Knowing that allowed me to make smart marketing decisions that my competition was too cheap to look at, such as offering guarantees, extra bonuses and incentives to attract clients, and "thank-you" referral gifts for clients who sent business our way.

So, if you have been in business for more than a couple of years, you should be able to calculate the lifetime value of your customers/

clients/ patients. You can always re-adjust it in a few years when you have more data to work with.

If you are brand new to your business, you will have to check out what the industry "norms" are, and use that to base your L.T.V. assumptions on. With proper marketing, service, and on-going contact, you can probably do a lot better than that – but it is a good place to start from.

The simple calculation for Lifetime Value is:

Average amount spent with you X average # of times they purchase from you X average length of the business relationship = Gross Sale amount.

For me, to calculate the Gross NET, I take out the "hard costs" of delivering my product or service (i.e. direct labour and product costs) but NOT my normal overhead (as that gets spent whether I have a customer or not).

So, let's say your hard costs are 50%. You then subtract that from your Gross Revenue to obtain your the Gross Net.

Give away a bit to gain a LOT.

Knowing the Lifetime Value of a client now allows you to make smarter marketing choices because it takes out the emotion and allows you to focus on the numbers.

So if you now know that an "average" customer is worth $10,000.00 to your business over a 3 year period, how will that affect how you treat them when they are in your business? How about how your staff treat them? Maybe you will start to monitor that a bit better, eh?

But it also shows you how much you should be willing to invest in order to acquire a new customer, and how much you should be willing to invest to keep one that is on the verge of leaving.

So if some of your marketing gets you a client at, let's say, an average of $700.00 per new client, and another marketing strategy gets you one at $1,000.00 per new client, what should you do?

Most people would cut the $1,000 option out and only focus on the $700 and quit doing the $1,000 one. I would suggest that you keep doing both (and as much of the $700 one as you can) because the $1,000 option is still a very good return on your investment.

If I told you, "give me $1,000 and I'll give you $10,000 back over the next 3 years" and you knew it was a sure thing, you'd be all over that deal as much as you could. That's a 1,000% return on investment for you over 3 years. 333.33% a year! Sure as hell beats what you get at the bank isn't it?

So, once you know what the Lifetime Value of your client is, and you track your marketing and know how much it costs you to get a new client with it, then the whole process is very simple...

If it works, keep doing it!

Dave Dubeau began his infatuation with marketing while living in San Jose, Costa Rica. By learning and implementing effective direct response marketing, he was able to take his start-up company from the bottom of the pack to the top three (with over 50 competitors) in 2.5 years.

Upon returning to Canada in 2003 with his Costa Rican wife, Susy, and their two kids, Amy and Andrew, Dave continued to put his marketing skills to good use – first in the field of "Creative Real Estate Investing", where he did "18 flips in 18 months", then with an advertising business, and later as a marketing consultant.

Dave really came into his own as a bona-fide marketing expert when he began working with "Canadian Rich Dad", Darren Weeks. Together they created the *Fast Track Inner Circle* membership program, and Dave eventually became the "Marketing Guy" for Darren's Fast Track group of companies. Dave began a whole new marketing focus for the companies, helped to quadruple the database from 15,000 to over 60,000 event attendees, and helped the companies to grow to $100M in gross annual sales.

Dave is a firm believer in on-going education and he invests tens of thousands of dollars a year going to a variety of marketing conferences, seminars and mastermind group meetings (many through the prestigious Glazer-Kennedy organization).

Dave's company is appropriately called **Results Enterprises Inc**. and is based out of Kamloops, British Columbia in Canada.

If you would like more information about Dave Dubeau and what he does, please visit **www.ResultsEnterprises.com**

Notes & Thoughts!

A BRIGHT IDEA

RETAIL MARKETING FOR PROFITS
Every Canadian Marketer's Guide
By D.J. Richoux

DJ Richoux is a marketer who I had heard a lot about before I got to meet him. His name came up quite often in the "Dan Kennedy" world of marketers, as he was one of Dan's original Mastermind attendees.

When I finally met DJ in person, I found him to be a very down-to-earth fellow and a lot of fun to associate with.

If you own a traditional "Brick and Mortar" business, this chapter is exactly for you. And if you don't, you should read it anyway because what DJ teaches can be used with any business.

~ Dave Dubeau

Not too long ago, I received a call from my sister's friend, Dan.

Dan is a driven 33-year-old entrepreneur with a burning desire to own his own business. He has always been a hard worker, juggling 2 jobs while working on some kind of business. I don't really know him that well, except that we previously met once or twice at social gatherings.

Over the phone, I could sense the tension and worry in his voice. He wanted to get together for a coffee. So we met at my favourite local coffee shop and sat in the corner in a couple of comfortable brown worn wingback leather chairs. Dan was a little uncomfortable, moving around in his chair, and a worrisome look in his eyes said it all. He wanted to get something off his chest – badly.

"Dan, what's happening?" I asked.

"DJ, thanks for meeting with me", he responded quickly. "Your sister tells me that you help retailers with their marketing to make their stores more profitable".

"That's right", I told him. And that's all it took for Dan to start pouring his heart out about his latest business venture.

"DJ, I had this great idea to open a hobby store that sells radio-controlled cars, trucks, and airplanes - basically anything radio-controlled. Through networking, I negotiated a great deal from two of the biggest suppliers in the radio control industry. I researched the market and decided to open a state-of-the-art 1,500 sq.ft. retail location with three different race courses, including an off-road course.

"I found a great unit on the main floor of a retail office building with big picture windows located at a busy intersection with high foot traffic as well as drive-by traffic and lots of parking in the area. It took me 11 weeks to find this location. I negotiated hard on the lease for another three weeks. I am probably paying 10 to 15% too much for the lease but…

**"I was told the key to retail success is
Location, Location, Location!"**

"I borrowed money from my parents to build and renovate the store. I opened six weeks late... I wouldn't even tell you about all those nightmares.

"I was totally pumped at the Grand Opening of my store. All my friends, parents and family were there to wish me the best. My parents had a gleam in their eye; you could tell they were proud of me. My friends told me that I had finally made it... that this was the one". There was a buzz in the air, and you could feel the energy in the store.

"Sales were good for the first month or so, but then I started noticing the store traffic was slowing down. My cash register wasn't ringing. It's been 3 months and I am not generating enough sales to even pay for my overhead, let alone myself".

"What should I do?" Dan asked. "Can you help?"

In my years of consulting and mentoring small to medium sized retailers, I have seen and heard many things.

Dan's scenario is what I call:

The "Hope Method" of Marketing

Many retailers believe that all you need to do is come up with a great and exciting store concept, find a great location, and hope customers will come to your store.

There was a time when a great location usually meant success. These days, however, you need more than just a great location and store concept.

Too many retailers open stores without any sound strategy or plans on how they are going to get customers.

What Every Retailer Needs is a Steady Flow of Profitable Customers Hungry for their Products

There are only three ways to grow a business. Any business activity falls into one of the three ways. These three methods are:

Method # 1: **Acquire _MORE_ New Customers**
Method # 2: **Have Your Customers Return _MORE OFTEN_**
Method # 3: **Have Your Customers _SPEND MORE_ Each Visit**

Many retailers understand the concept of getting more new customers. They run many promotions such as newspaper ads, radio ads, newspaper inserts/ flyers, maybe direct mail, Val Pak and other kinds of promotions. They use and understand Method # 1.

Did you know? Studies have confirmed that attracting new customers cost retailers more than attracting existing customers to come back. Many surveys have also shown that customers who have shopped in a store before will spend, on average twice as much as any first time customer.

> **'Acquiring a new customer costs _six to seven times more_ than retaining one'**
>
> ~ Frederick Reichheld
>   VP at consultants Bain & Co. in Boston & author of _The Loyalty Effect_

This is truly ground-breaking because it shows that Method # 2 and # 3 are really where the big profits are! It is far easier and cheaper to get a customer to return to your store than it is to get a new customer. It costs more to win a new customer than keep an existing one.

It is important for retailers to spend their initial advertising dollars to attract new customers (Method # 1). But the real profits are in what you do with these new customers AFTER you've acquired them. Retailers need a system to gather information from their customers so they can market to them in the future, transitioning them from new one-time customers to repeat clients, because returning customers keep on buying!

It's that simple!

The Key to Retail Profits = Generate More Sales from Your Customer Base

But it's not really a retailer's fault.

They were never taught that the key to retail success is building a relationship with their customers so those customers would come in more often and spend more in their store. Their college marketing class or marketing diploma only gave them theoretical concepts on how to build a business using factors such as location, product pricing, promotions across different channels etc. and only brushed the tip of the surface on dealing with customers and more importantly...

Mining Your Customer Base to More Retail Profits!

Most have no understanding on how to do this!

Every retailer should "touch" (contact) their customers at least every 21 days through some form of communication. Ideally you should be contacting your customers 24 to 30 or more times a year. I recommend contacting them at least once a month by mail and an additional 1 to 4 times a month by email. You need to be in constant contact with your customers as their lives are busy with their circumstances changing all the time. You need to contact them on a regular basis to give them a good reason to come to your store and also so they don't forget about you.

For those of you who don't contact your customers, you may think that my recommendation is a little far fetched. In fact, you may be thinking…

Is there such a thing as "over-contacting" my customer base?

The Reality is 98.2 % of Retailers Don't Contact Their Customers Enough!

What retailers don't realize is that each year, their customer base is shrinking from one or more of the following factors:

- Some of your customers pass away
- Some of your customers move away
- Some of your customers have a lifestyle change and become unemployed or get divorced
- Some of your customers are lured away by a competitor
- Some of your customers simply forget about you

This shrinking customer base is best illustrated by the leaky marketing bucket shown here.

FACT: If retailers do not do anything, they will lose 25%-50% of their customers every year.

© 2005-2009 Firepower Marketing Inc.

The GOOD NEWS is that I teach retailers that they need to plug their holes in their leaky marketing bucket and create a marketing funnel.

What's a Marketing Funnel?

Like the picture of the funnel below, a marketing funnel is wide at the top and narrow at the bottom.

© 2005-2009 Firepower Marketing Inc.

You want all your customers to enter the top of your marketing funnel. You then continue to market to them by using direct mail and email, for example. Now when those one-time customers come back to your store they are becoming repeat clients. As those clients come more often and spend more in your retail store, they move down your funnel by being frequent purchasers. You are now

187

building a stronger relationship with them and giving them more value, so your store profitability increases.

Not everyone will reach the bottom of your funnel, but your best clients will. I call your best clients your "guests" as you want to treat your best clients as "guests" in your store.

The More You Connect with Your Customers…
The More Profits You will See!

Frederick Reichheld, author of *The Loyalty Effect* and a VP at the Bain & Co. consulting firm in Boston, studied the effects that customer retention and loyalty had on a business. He said the following:

> **'An Increase in Customer Retention of 5% will yield an increase in profits of 25%-100%.'**
>
> ~ Frederick Reichheld

Imagine being able to turn a one-time sales transaction with a new customer into a long term repeat customer who visits your store more often, and spends more each time!

The key to retail profits is to sell more products and services to your existing customers. Your goal is to have 10 to 20 per cent of your customers become long-term repeat customers… and doing this will put more retails profits in your pocket.

This is best captured by the following **Retail Profit Pyramid**:

Retail Profit Pyramid™

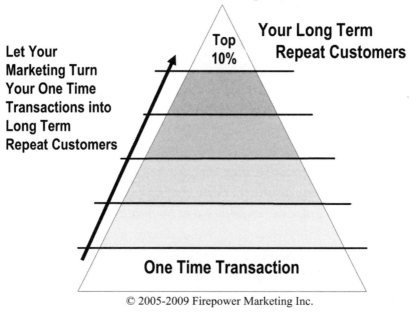

Let Your Marketing Turn Your One Time Transactions into Long Term Repeat Customers

Top 10%

Your Long Term Repeat Customers

One Time Transaction

© 2005-2009 Firepower Marketing Inc.

So where's the breakdown?

Despite knowing that customers are the # 1 reason why retailers stay in business or go flat broke, many of them struggle with cost-effective ways to attract new customers and are consistently challenged with how to bring back existing customers. They just don't have a system in place to bring existing customers back into the store on a regular basis.

Retailers, in general, struggle with customer retention for these reasons:

1. They do NOT have an "iron clad" system of customer data collection.

189

2. They do NOT communicate enough with their pre-sent customers in multiple ways.
3. They do NOT track lost customers and so don't communicate with them.
4. They do NOT update their customer database (list).
5. They do NOT properly segment their customers.

Do a quick recall here:

- *When you last visited your favourite retail store and paid for your purchase, did they ask for your contact information such as name, address, email, and phone number?*
- *Does that store ever contact you by phone or mail?*
- *Does that store ever send you a Thank You note, a birthday card, gift certificate or an awards letter?*

So how do retailers break out of this rut? My answer to this is to start implementing a…

Proven Retail Marketing Loyalty System that Will Bring Back Existing Customers as Well as Attract New Customers

A great retail marketing system uses such proven database marketing strategies as direct mail and email with the power and leverage of a loyalty program.

Retailers use loyalty programs for two main goals. The primary goal is to gain information relating to their customers' spending habits. The secondary goal is to ensure customers continue to patronize their business.

Everyone has, or belongs to, one or more loyalty programs. Just take a peek in your wallet. Do you have a Petro-Points card, a Staples Dividend Card, a Sears Club Points, iRewards from Chapters, or HBC Rewards Points card? I could go on and on.

According to the COLLOQUY Research, there are over 114 million active Canadian loyalty memberships.

(Source: *The Financial Post*, Tuesday, April 14, 2009)

In Canada, the oldest loyalty program was initiated by Canadian Tire. Customers were given Canadian Tire money, coupons which look like currency. Originally given for gas purchases only, as of 1961, coupons have been presented with all purchases at Canadian Tire stores, and today they can be used to make non-gas, in-store purchases, as well as to buy automotive services.

Today, loyalty programs are everywhere. They are available to grocery stores such as Superstore, Loblaws, or Save-On-Foods. Gas stations such as Esso, Petro Canada, and Chevron also have loyalty programs. Even hotels like Sheraton, Best Western, Hilton, and Marriott offer some sort of loyalty program. Of course, the big retail stores are not missing out on the power of loyalty programs. Staples Business Depot has its Dividends Card, and Chapters has its iRewards program – just to name a few.

From these examples, one can too quickly conclude that only big, established retailers can afford to profit wildly from a loyalty program. But...

Loyalty Programs are NOT just for the "Big Chains"!

I am seeing small independent retailers as well as medium-sized retailers benefit greatly from implementing a loyalty program in their business.

One of the clients with whom I consult is Alan Glasser of Mark's Pharmacy. Using the loyalty program I recommended to him, his pharmacy has doubled retail sales from $128,000 to $273,000. He only has 250 sq. ft. retail sales area. (I'll tell you more about Mark's Pharmacy success story later on...).

Just remember this...

Any Canadian marketer not playing the loyalty game is at a competitive disadvantage.

(Source: Colloquy White Paper, *The Canadian Difference*, October 2007)

Steal Your Customers Back from National Chains – Fight Back with a Retail Marketing Loyalty System!

Here are 13 of the most important features retailers need to look for when considering a retail marketing loyalty system or program:

1. **Loyalty Membership cards (preferably plastic) promoting your store.** When your customers carry your loyalty membership card in their wallets, they are more likely to remember you. Everyone reaches into their wallets regularly to buy things. Membership cards provide you with continued exposure, and studies have shown that repeated exposure leads to an increase in potential customer purchase.

2. **Easy to understand and implement.** The loyalty program should be easy to show and explain to your customers. Make sure you train your employees on the system. Have your employees practice a sign-up script and get them to role play with each other. Make refinements to the sign-up script as needed. You should ask every customer in your store to sign-up for your loyalty program.

   It is also a good idea to start an incentive program for your employees for enrolling customers into your loyalty program. Incentives could be given for meeting a daily enrolment target or a weekly quota, whichever works best for you.

3. **Attractive in-store signage that encourages YOUR customers to sign-up for Your Loyalty program.** This can be signage strategically placed by your cash register, front door/ window, community announcement board, or washrooms, basically any high traffic area for the sole purpose of maximizing exposure. You want your customers to know that you have a loyalty program!

4. **Built-in referral program.** Customers will refer their friends and associates to your business for FREE. These

referred customers tend to be better long-term customers. A good loyalty program needs to be able to identify these referrals for you. It is best to give some kind of incentive to the customer who refers a friend or associate to your business. It can be just a small incentive to acknowledge to your customer that you appreciated and recognized that they referred a friend.

5. **A program that runs 100% on auto-pilot after the customer is a member of your program.** By automatic, I mean ongoing monthly mail and email communication with your customer to keep him coming back more often. For instance, after your customer has signed up for your loyalty program, your customer should receive some sort of welcome letter or postcard. Your customers should also get, for example, birthday cards and anniversary cards. You want a program that pulls the data and mails the birthday cards automatically every month for you. You don't have the time to mail 20 to 50 birthday cards every month.

Here is a tip: Focus your time and your staff's time on signing up customers to your loyalty program. This is the best use of your time. A good loyalty program should allow you to focus 90% of your time to signing up new customers.

6. **Seasonal and promotional mailings.** Your retail marketing loyalty system should allow you the option of mailing optional and seasonal promotion each and every month to your customers. Think about holidays such as Easter, St Patrick's Day, Halloween, Canada Day, Valentine's Day, Back to School etc.

Some customers may be more responsive to email invite-ations. One of the challenges with email is deliverability. Too often the email does not get to your customer. I will guarantee you, however, that your customers will appreciate the personal touch of receiving a letter or postcard. They will let you know by bringing in the mailing and spending money in the store or business.

I like a program that uses large full-color postcards to make sure you get your customers' attention.

7. **Powerful email program with flexibility.** The system you choose should use an email system that allows you send out custom HTML and standard text emails, while tracking open and click through rates automatically. It should also be able to integrate with special and optional direct mail campaigns. This way, you will have more effective email campaigns that will increase your sales and profits.

8. **Personalized Direct Mail and Email.** We all like to read and hear our name. That is why it increases response by at least 30%. It is best to personalize with first and last name. I also like to use a full color large postcard to make sure I get their attention. Treat your customers with personalization and call them by name in your store and you will have taken a positive step forward to turning your customers into clients, and some of those clients will become long time guests of your business.

9. **Real Time Reporting.** You want the ability to track and see your results immediately. Your loyalty program should be able to generate reports such as:

- Total Number Of Members
- Total Member Sign-Ups By Month
- Sales Year-To-Date
- Sales By Month
- Birthdays Next Month
- Top Percentage Of Customers By $ Amount
- Top Percentage Of Customers By Visit Frequency
- Etc. Etc. Etc.

Reports help you stay in-tune with the health and the pulse of your business. You can start tracking trends and weaknesses in your business. Reports are another set of eyes watching your business for you. Your loyalty program needs to have the capability of running multiple standard reports as well as custom reports.

10. **Customized promotional offers and specials.** Your retail marketing loyalty system should have a feature that allows you to change an offer or special on a mailing or email remotely via the internet. You want a feature that is easy to use and learn. Ideally you want to be able update or change a special in less than 5 minutes.

With real time reporting, you can quickly look at the results of a weekly email or internet special. If the results are below average, you can quickly change your special or offer.

11. **Customer and member survey options**. Your system needs to be able to provide you with valuable feedback from your customers. You need to have the option to do customer and member surveys quickly and easily.

You can use the positive feedback you get from your customers in your marketing. You will also get valuable feedback on how your employees are interacting with your customers.

12. **Database segmentation.** Your retail marketing loyalty system has to have the ability to segment your customer database. This is the GOLD MINE I have been referring to. We all know that all customers are not created equal. They have different spending habits. Some spend more than others. Some visit once every a month or so, some visit every two weeks; others visit your store even more often.

Different segments of your clients will respond to different types of marketing and with different promotions and offers. One way to identify your customers is by segmentation. You want to segment your list by purchase behaviour, frequency, and sales. This way, you SAVE MONEY knowing who your best clients are, and what type of marketing they respond to. Instead of randomly spending your advertising dollars with advertisers that don't under-stand your customers' buying habits, you now will know where to attract similar customers with similar demographics to your business.

Bottom line, with list segmentation, you increase your profits with lower costs!

13. **Automatic customer database cleaning.** "Cleaning" your customer database, means using Address Standardization, NCOA (National Change of Address) and Merge/ Purge (duplication elimination) to keep your customer database up to date. We all know that some of our customers move,

change email addresses, and change jobs etc. A good loyalty program ensures that your database is up to date. Your promotions and mailings are delivered only to those with good addresses, which means you get better results with lower costs.

I'll wrap up this chapter by showcasing Alan Glasser, the small independent retailer who has used a retail marketing loyalty system and is seeing amazing results.

How a Small Independent Retailer battles National Chains with a Retail Marketing Loyalty System and WINS!

Alan Glasser is a typical, 55-year-old hardworking retailer who has been in the retail business for 30 years. Glasser is a pharmacist and retail store owner of Mark's Pharmacy, which has only 250 square feet of retail space in Delta, BC.

Like many other independent retail store owners, he used to get nervous when a Costco, Loblaws or Super Store opened in the area with all their bells and whistles, and big budget flyers and promotions... anything to steal his customers.

Glasser realized that he needed to invest time into looking for the most effective tools and systems to grow his business. "I realized that everything changes. My business... my customers and clients... my competition! I needed to be innovative and keep up with the times," Glasser said. "If I stubbornly refuse to adapt to the 'new emerging economy', my business will slowly die. A lost customer here, a new competitor there, and soon I'd have to close the doors."

Then one day, he discovered an innovative and somewhat unconventional customer marketing loyalty system.

Although sceptical, he tried it out and was stunned with the results!

Using this system, Glasser confirms that his average square foot sales have increased to $685 per square foot – 50% higher than the industry standard! In the past year alone, his pharmacy has experienced a 30 percent increase in PROFITS from prescription sales, with a 350% increase in sales of his key product line, alternative health products dealing with pain. 52 out of every 100 people who received a certain promotion came in and purchased something.

He made $57 for every $1 spent on a campaign to bring back "lost" customers. In the last 3 months alone, Glasser has increased sales by an average of 30% per month over year. Since he took over the pharmacy 5 years ago, his retail sales have increased by 8 times.

When I drove out to his Delta store to conduct this interview and confirm his results, I was shocked at the size of his store – his retail space is a tiny 250 sq. ft.! It's smaller than a typical bachelor pad!

I asked him the obvious question, "How can a small local retailer compete and win against the big stores like Loblaws, Costco, Superstore etc in today's new economy? What's your secret?"

"The True Secret to Success is Generating More Sales from My Existing Customer Base"

Glasser's answer was simple. "The true secret to success is generating more sales from my existing customer base", he told me. "Advertising can be expensive, but building a solid relationship and loyalty with my current customers is low-cost and highly profitable."

He goes on to say how using a proven customer marketing loyalty system, he now proudly lists the names of his top 100 customers! He even knows that his average customer has spent around $180 in his store in the last 6 months.

He emphasizes, "Every dollar I spend in marketing and advertising should give me a good return." He is getting an unheard of return of $37.00 or more for every dollar he spends in advertising.

"Advertising and marketing should not be an expense. It should be an investment that brings me back loyal customers and profits. And this customer loyalty program is a MUST HAVE if anyone is serious about growing their retail business."

It's no wonder he's not devastated by the growth of Costco, Loblaws or Superstore. They can't touch him – nor can they steal his customers!

It's Time YOU Start Using a Retail Marketing Loyalty System

By now, you understand the undeniable power of a retail marketing loyalty system program and how profitable it is. A small independent retailer like Alan Glasser has done it!

If you are serious about increasing your retail store profits, you need to be using some kind of loyalty program, preferably a retail marketing loyalty system.

Today – immediately – start capturing your customer's information!

Then do the following steps:

1. Create a Loyalty Program
2. Design Marketing Pieces
3. Take them to the Printer
4. Address & Stamp the Postcards
5. Hire Extra Staff to Manage the Additional Workload
6. Hire Tech Support to Integrate Database Software with the mailing software
7. Repeat Again and Again for:
   - Birthdays and Anniversaries every month
   - Random Award letters, welcome and Thank-you cards
   - Quarterly Statements every three months
   - Email Reminders weekly, monthly, special promotion
   - Special Occasion and Seasonal Promotions every month

Or if you just want the whole thing done for you, check out **http://www.RetailMarketingForProfits.com**

I wish you the best of success!

DJ Richoux specializes in finding the "hidden profits" in small to medium-sized retail businesses. DJ combines his practical "street-smart" customer service, and his retail marketing skills and training with his University Degree in Business Administration (with a concentration on marketing). DJ comes from a retail background, spending eight years taking care of Jaguar, Land Rover and Porsche customers, where he won numerous customer service awards. When DJ left his career in the retail industry, he was a Service Manager for a Porsche dealership.

Since then, DJ has worked with small to medium-sized independent retailers in many different niches, including franchise owners of The Medicine Shoppe® and The UPS Stores®. DJ is passionate about helping business owners create sustainable, profitable growth in their businesses. DJ remains a busy, sought after business/ retail mentor and consultant, due to his unique ability to uncover little known profitable strategies that any small business owner can use to skyrocket their income.

To learn more go to: **www.RetailMarketingForProfits.com**

FREE Gift Offer! Get over $595.00 in additional marketing and business building special reports, audio CD's and DVD's mailed right to your door. See page 271 for complete details, or visit: **www.ResultsEnterprises.com/gift.html**

YOUR MILLION DOLLAR NETWORK
How Building Relationships is Key to Your Success
By July Ono

I met July Ono when I first returned to Canada. We were both at a T. Han Easter event and she was just getting started in her real estate marketing business. We met, exchanged business cards, and July followed up with me within 24 hours. She had 3 "doors" when I first met her and at the time of this book she is up to 400 plus "doors" in her portfolio.

Her key to success is her amazing follow up and contact system.

What she does with her monthly email continuity program is applicable to any kind of business – including yours.   Read and enjoy!

~ Dave Dubeau

Relationships are the master key to riches. Wherever you see successful people, there are successful relationships that laid the foundation for their success. It is how well we connect and inter-connect with people that determine how successful our outcome is.

If you don't have a continuity program, a continuous way of staying in touch with your network, then chances are you are struggling in life. *Your Million Dollar Network* is a system that is strategically designed to cultivate your social network so you can monetize your return on investment.

Have you considered what it costs you to find a new client? Advertising in newspapers and magazines to a broad audience will produce, on average, a 1% to 3% response ratio. And that's just a response. This is not actual sales.

The best return on your investment is obtained by marketing to your existing clients. You will receive, on average, a 65% return on investment. And your existing clients will bring in new customers through word-of-mouth, still by far the most powerful form of advertising. Third party referrals have enormous credibility.

Everybody seems to know the "why". We all know that net-working is important. It's the "how" that is elusive. This chapter is devoted to an overview of how you can tap into your network and start getting results.

When you meet someone you have never met before, are you waiting for them to finish saying their blurb so you can blurt out yours? This is just an exercise in making noise. Networking is about connecting with people. It is about being sincere, authentic, and genuine. The intention is to help, give value, and empower others. And it starts with listening.

From now on, when you meet someone, and you exchange business cards, you are to write down three things you heard them say not related to their business card.

Did they go skiing over the weekend? Are they planning a trip? Did they just have a baby? Do they like pets? What is their favourite gardening activity? Do they love a particular type of restaurant? Are they a wine connoisseur? Do they enjoy quilting or crochet or art? Do they play tennis or soccer? How many children do they have? Write down anything, except what they do for a living. Their profession, career, or job, does not define who that person is. And this is not how you are going to make that special connection. Because in life everything is personal.

It's when you are able to influence their social behaviour, not just their corporate façade, that one-on-one connection really takes hold. And this is the most powerful form of connection there is.

The next most powerful success habit is following up. Listen to what they are sharing. Follow up within twenty-four hours, and mention one, two, or all three of those non-related items in your correspondence. The idea is to add value to their lives. Can you solve a problem for them? Can you direct them to a resource? I remember one conversation with a person who was experiencing vertigo due to a chronic neck injury. I connected him with a specialized chiropractor in my network who does not "crack" the spine, he presses. How do I know? He fixed my vertigo in one session after a car accident.

Building relationships and creating your network is all about leverage. The leverage I am referring to is OPM (other people's money), OPT (other people's time) and OPR (other people's resources).

The more people you have in your network, the more potential leverage you have. But you need a system to tap into your network that produces results.

This system is thoroughly explained in my book *Your Million Dollar Network: how to start and build a million dollar network* available at **www.yourmilliondollarnetworkbook.com**.

It's not about collecting as many business cards as you can, although you can do that. Is it working for you? This is where leverage comes to the rescue. All you really need to do is focus on your core two hundred relationships to let the *three degrees of separation* work their magic for you.

The average person knows approximately two hundred people. I started strategic networking with twenty people in my database, and this number has grown to four thousand over seven years. However, I still have a core two hundred people I am closest to. I call this core group my "immediate circle of influence". Everybody has an "immediate circle of influence".

So if we can agree that the average person has an average network of two hundred people, then we can take this logic to the first degree of separation: the friends of your friends. This means that if two hundred people in your "immediate circle of influence" know two hundred people, that's 200 x 200 = 40,000. That's forty thousand people that you can potentially connect to in your first degree of separation. That's a lot of people, a lot of connections, and a lot of resources just waiting to be tapped into.

We can take this logic to the second degree of separation: the friends of the friends of your "immediate circle of influence". That's 40,000 x 200 = 8,000,000. That's eight million people in your second degree of separation!

Now it gets kind of crazy because in the third degree of separation, the friends of the friends of the friends of your "immediate circle of influence", that's 8,000,000 x 200 = 1.6 billion people.

There's no such thing as a fourth degree of separation because that number exceeds the population of the planet. You are literally connected to everybody on the planet, indirectly perhaps, through your core two hundred relationships. Can you see the power of your network?

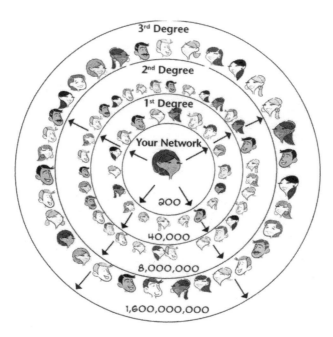

Now you need a plan.

Strategic networking is like baseball. We all start at home plate with business cards in hand and go out to networking events. Most people don't even get off home plate. Hey, the ball is coming at you and you've got to take a swing.

You get to first base by taking a swing, talking to someone, making a connection, exchanging business cards, or writing down three things about them not related to their business card. This is your initial contact, so follow up with them immediately. This one simple act of following up will set you apart from the masses mired in mediocrity.

You get to second base by repeatedly using the Convincer Strategy and the Motivation Strategy to enrol, engage, and invite these new relationships into your life on a continuous

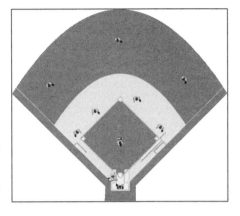

basis. When sufficient value has been exchanged, this will result in a value exchange of money, time or resources.

You get to third base when the value exchange has taken place. And this is where most people stop. They've spent all this work and effort in getting a sale or a referral or a contract, and they move on to the next one. If you were playing baseball, you may have run the bases, but you're not even on the scoreboard yet.

You need to get a home run. When you are a strategic networker, you are building a million dollar network, and the only way to accomplish this is by cultivating an army of evangelists. These people praise the good news about you, your company, your business, your goods, your products, your services, your website. They share you with everyone they know. They bring business to you. Talk about unsolicited advertising and promotion on your behalf! You can't get them to shut up about you even if you paid them to. This is the awesome result you can achieve when you create so much value in other people's lives that they can't help but share your goodness with others.

This means it is wise to cultivate an impeccable reputation. Good news travels fast; bad news travels faster. Beware of short-term gain at the expense of long-term relationships. Core values in business are all about personal core values. People pay attention to businesses run by successful people because at the heart of the business is an entrepreneur, business owner, or proprietor who will not compromise on their values.

Communicating your core values takes time. Time and repetition are integral to building strong relationships. So how can you build strong relationships with lots of people when there are only so many hours in a day? This is where you need a networking stand-in.

In the movie industry, they use a stand-in actor who resembles the hero actor who is usually the highest paid. Why waste money on blocking and lighting with the hero actor when a stand-in will suffice at a substantially lower cost? In the same way, it is time consuming and labour intensive to meet-and-greet people in person. There are only so many lunches and dinners that you can do. So your newsletter acts like your stand-in. And from my experience, and the experience of a lot of people who have used this networking system, the results are outstanding.

A simple newsletter written in a casual format sent out once a month is all that is required to build, maintain, and attract people, money, and opportunities. Done consistently over time, your network receives the message at the unconscious level that you are credible, dependable, reliable, and trustworthy. You always show up. You stand out from the crowd and this makes you exceptional and worthy of notice.

It all comes down to trust. People trust consistency and predictability. If you're hit-and-miss in business, then you're going to attract hit-and-miss clients. This is a law of the universe: You attract what you put out. By all means, give value first, and you will attract value. You are not in business for a sales transaction. You are in business for a lifetime of value transactions. The lifetime value of just one person is priceless. So get connected and stay connected. There's a saying that goes, "you never get a second chance to make a first impression". That's baloney. True networking is all about making a lasting impression. And follow up, follow up, follow up.

July Ono currently owns and manages a $30+ million commercial real estate portfolio. A real estate investor, educator and entrepreneur, July is the President of On The Beach Education® Corporation. Her company offers a coaching and mentoring program designed to take the fear out of real estate investing. Their goal is to help people leverage proven systems, to achieve their financial independence, sooner than later. Between 2006 to 2008, her students have acquired over $40 million of investment properties.

She has a passion for networking and empowering others to live their potential. She strongly believes that applied knowledge is power and that this is the path to enlightenment and financial freedom.

July's single-minded determination to succeed led her to develop systems and tools to help her clients and students succeed in business. On The Beach Education® Corporation was launched to help share her knowledge and discoveries with people who want to succeed in business.

July is a multi-talented woman with a host of interests that span from running triathlons to screenwriting. She is a PADI certified scuba diver; black belt instructor in Taekwondo; small calibre marksman; and a speed typist clocked at over 115 words per minute.

July has also been a professional actor and screenwriter. Her on screen credits include a host of commercials, independent films and the award winning Harvest Production/National Film Board production of *"Obachan's Garden"*.

July enjoys spending time in sunny Tsawwassen with her husband when she is not travelling the world looking for new investment property, teaching seminars or playing an exotic new sport.

Notes & Thoughts!

SEVEN HUGELY-PROFITABLE INTERNET BUSINESS MODELS YOU CAN COPY AND PROFIT FROM TODAY

By Dan Lok

Dan 'the Man" Lok is an amazing fellow who I met in 2007 though Brandon Roe. Dan and I hit it off quickly. Due to his great experience with copy writing, and offline and online marketing, I asked him to become a contributing writer for both of my newsletter publications – FTIC and BC Profit$.

Dan's a very sharp marketer and when it comes to online marketing, he really knows his stuff. If you are curious about how to apply the Internet to your business more effectively, you will enjoy this chapter.

~ David Dubeau

The other day, I was on an airplane, sitting next to a man who told me he owned three "famous name" fast food outlets, each grossing over a million dollars a year – and he hated the business!

He went on to explain that after making the loan payments on the huge sum he'd put up to get into the business, paying the franchise fees and royalties, advertising and employees, his "net" income was less than $300,000 a year. He also told me the employee headaches alone were driving him crazy; they quit without notice, didn't show up, stole, showed up drunk, and fought with each other in the parking lot!

He then asked me about my business.

I told him I had no employee headaches… had just about every detail of the business "outsourced" or "automated"… make my money via email and websites… have money coming in even while I sleep, watch TV, or go on vacations and do less gross than he does, but keep a lot more of the money.

He said he had over $2,000,000.00 borrowed and tied up in his stores, equipment and franchises, and he asked how much it cost to get a business like mine going. I told him that I got started with less than $10,000.

If there's so much money to be made on the internet, why do so many business owners fail to make a fortune online?

I believe one of the things that keeps many entrepreneurs from making big money online is LACK OF FOCUS.

Often the thing preventing even people who are already making money online from going to the next level, from making that quantum leap, is lack of focus.

Nowadays we are so easily distracted. I am surprised and shocked at how often entrepreneurs get sucked into these "opportunities" and hyped-up sales pitches. Every day, we all get inundated with a ton of e-mails and various offers.

So we buy this product, we buy this e-book, and we think we're going to find the answer that we're looking for. So this month, we're doing this particular business opportunity, next month were doing something else. I see this as the biggest problem holding people back.

I've often said that the most powerful form of business knowledge is business models. If you have a model for a system that works, you can use it to spawn countless ideas and projects. So that's why I want to talk about 7 different widely profitable business models that you can copy and profit from.

Over the past 6 years I've worked behind the scenes with dozens of the successful internet entrepreneurs, and watched them pull in millions of dollars... and they all did it using one or more of these business models.

Now, you might recognize some of these business models; you might know them or have heard of them, but it will be worth reviewing them.

And perhaps I will expose you to some different business models you have never heard of. This will expand your horizons, and just maybe give you a fresh perspective on how these models work.

You see, people get confused. They think that since "I'm selling this particular product... or I'm selling this particular service" that they have a business, when in fact, this is not quite a business – it's just a product.

A business model is entirely different. And the funny thing is most people don't even have a business model. You ask them what their business model is, and they cannot tell you what it is or how it works.

Years ago, my mentor said to me, "If you cannot put your business model on a napkin and explain it in two minutes or less, you don't have a business".

You should be very clear about how your business model works, what you're doing to bring in the leads, and how you're making money. So, with that, let's talk about business model number one...

Proven Money-Making Model # 1 – Affiliate Marketing

One of the questions I'm asked most often is, "Dan, how do I get started? I don't have a lot of money. I'm just a beginner, and I want to start making money online. What would you recommend that I do?"

My reply is always affiliate marketing. I believe affiliate marketing is one of the easiest ways to get started making money on Internet.

First of all, let me explain exactly what affiliate marketing is: It's nothing more than no-risk partnership. You promote other people's products and services on your web site, on your blog, on your list – and when the visitors you send to them actually buy their product or service, you will get paid a percentage of the profit.

So, in a way, think of yourself as a middleman who is selling other company's products and services to get paid a commission. That's the easiest way to explain it.

Now, most of the time, when you're just getting started, affiliate marketing is so easy because you can get started in just days, and get started making money within days after that.

Think about it. If you start developing your own products, you have to deal with inventory, fulfillment, customer support – all the things that go with an Internet business. It can be overwhelming, especially if you're just getting started. With affiliate marketing, you have none of those headaches to deal with. That's why affiliate marketing is such a fantastic way to get started.

Also, with affiliate marketing, you are promoting other people's products, so it allows you to focus all of your time and effort on one thing and one thing only – the marketing of the product. You get to spend the majority of your time driving traffic to the site of the product that you're promoting.

And if you picked the products and services correctly, meaning they have a:

- Good product
- Good track record
- Good sales process
- Good web site that converts visitors into customers

then it's relatively easy for you to start making money quickly.

Rosalind Gardner, a good friend of mine, has a dating site (**http://101date.com**) on which she does reviews of different dating sites and different dating advice sites on the Internet. She also promotes other dating sites. It's interesting, because all of these dating sites pay a recurring commission.

Rosalind actually makes hundreds of thousands of dollars a year promoting other people's products.

So, don't think of affiliate marketing as something to just make a little bit of money. It can be serious, and you can actually make quite a bit of money doing this. It's definitely a great way to get started.

Proven Money-Making Model # 2 – eBay

Another great way for beginners to get started is selling stuff on eBay. Maybe you have purchased or sold some things on eBay yourself. I know I have certainly bought a lot of things on eBay!

In case you don't know, let me give you some simple statistics about eBay. When you hear these statistics, you should get pretty excited about this particular business model:

+ eBay gets over 2 million visitors every day, searching for products to buy. Unlike people going to Google or various search engines searching for information, eBay visitors are buyers. They're looking for something specific, and they have money they want to spend.

♦ People spend an average of 1hr 47 minutes on eBay every time they visit. So that means they spent a lot of time on eBay just looking around for ways to spend money. Isn't that exciting?

♦ eBay currently has over 244 million members across the world, and their numbers are growing. They add thousands of new members every single day.

♦ Over $2000 in transactions per second go through eBay. That adds up to $86 million being spent every day on eBay.

In order to make money online, you need two things: traffic and conversion. So you need good quality, targeted traffic going to your web site, and you need a web site that converts in order to make money on the internet. It's pretty simple.

At eBay, the traffic is already there. They get millions of visitors every single day and you can tap into that for free. You can go to eBay.com, get an account and start selling within hours.

If you haven't sold anything online, what I would recommend is going through your basement or your garage to find some stuff that you don't want, you don't need, or something you've bought in the past that you no longer use. Now, just list them on eBay and see what happens.

Number one, not only are you turning your trash into cash, but you're also learning the process, how everything works along the way. It's very easy to use and it's very easy to list different products. If you just click on "Help", a lot of the information on how to do it is available for free through eBay.

Remember, eBay wants to teach you and wants you to learn how to sell effectively on eBay – the more you sell, the more they make. So eBay is not a bad business model if you're just getting started.

Proven Money-Making Model # 3 – Selling Ad Space

This model will work if you're getting a lot of traffic to your site, and you want to take advantage of that traffic and squeeze more money out of it. There are many advertisers who are willing to pay darn good money to get exposure for their offers and their web sites. So selling ad space is also an easy way for beginners to get started, because you don't have to ship anything, you don't have to deal with customer service, and you don't have to deal with products.

I have to say, though, this business model is not an easy way to make a huge profit, but if you are getting a huge amount of targeted traffic to your site, then yes, you can make a significant amount of money doing this.

Blog for Rent

An easy way to get started selling ad space is with a blog. You can set up a blog for free at **wordpress.com** or **blogger.com**. I do know a couple of bloggers who sell ad space on their site and they make anywhere from $5,000 to $10,000 a month – all with no products and no mailing list. All they have is a blog. So, it's not a bad way to get started at all.

The easiest way to do this is to start with Google AdSense (**www.google.com/adsense**) and sign up for an free account. You just place some small, tiny, relevant text ads on your site, and whenever a visitor clicks on one of these ads, you will get paid a small commission per click. AdSense is one of the easiest ways to get started.

If you're getting a lot of traffic, there are other ways to get paid through this business model. You can also sell banner advertising space, pop up ads, or text links.

If you have a list of newsletter subscribers, you can sell e-zine ads, and you could sell article space within your newsletter. If you are capturing leads on your site, you can actually sell those leads to other companies. For example, I know a marketer in the "how to get rich in real estate" niche who has captured names of people who are interested in getting rich in real estate. He sells the leads for $1 a pop.

He's making thousands and thousands of dollars every month just from selling those leads.

There are some Super AdSense marketers making in excess of $100,000 a month. However, these are the exceptions and certainly not the rule. But it can be done!

You can sell ad space on any one (or more) of the following:
- E-zines
- Blogs
- Directories
- Forums, discussion boards
- Blogs
- Search sites
- Social networking or bookmarking sites

Basically, anywhere where people will visit, you can sell space to put an ad in front of them.

Proven Money-Making Model # 4 – Lead Generation

Let's say you are a service provider, such as a consultant or a business coach, a copywriter, or even if you have an off-line business as, for example, a bookkeeper, freelancer, or graphic artist, the next model will work for you.

Basically, you're selling a service, but you're using the Internet as the way to generate the lead for your services, online or off-line.

It's pretty simple. With this business model, the purpose of your site would be to build trust, to position yourself as the expert, to build credibility, and to sell the visitors on who you are, what you do, and why they should contact you.

In a way, you're not actually making a direct sale on the site, because you don't actually have a way for them to make an immediate purchase.

Most of the time, what you would have would be a form on your site, and they would go there and fill out the form. Once they've filled out the form, you could call them or have them call you or you could e-mail them. Eventually you would close the sale over the phone – that's how this business model works.

Being a well-respected expert in your field gives you plenty of opportunities to make money. Not only can you sell the actual service that you provide, but the more you become respected as an expert, the more people will desire to pay you money to teach them what you do.

For instance, in the latter part of my copywriting career (I've now retired), I started to develop quite a name for myself, not only with my copywriting clients, but among other aspiring copywriters.

It was my well-respected position as an authority on the subject of copywriting that led naturally to the sale of my e-books & courses (all of which are still making money to this day), as well as becoming a coach and a consultant to other copywriters.

Another interesting angle: Use your website as a way to generate traffic for other coaches & consultants. Since there's only one "you", there's only so much one-on-one consulting and coaching you can do. If you have a well-marketed website, you're probably going to get more business that you can handle.

Instead of letting that business go to waste because you can't get to it, why not let other coaches and consultants in your niche advertise on your site?

Proven Money-Making Model # 5 – E-Commerce Sites

An e-commerce site is a catalogue site where you sell a variety of (most of the time physical) products on your web site. You might have dozens or even hundreds of products on your site.

Now with this model, you can do it one of these two ways:

1. Sell and ship your own products. Let's say you have an off-line business, such as a retail store. You have a lot of different, unique products, so you could easily just take a picture and post them on your e-commerce site and you could start marketing them. You're basically generating a new source of revenue through the Internet.

2. Drop-Shipping. If you're just getting started, and you don't want to stock and ship your own products, that's fine. That's where drop-shipping comes in. Do this if you don't want the hassles of tracking your own inventories, setting up a warehouse, shipping and receiving products, etc. Drop-shipping actually lets you sell quality name-brand products on your web site for a profit, while the drop-shipper takes care of fulfilling the order. It's not a bad way to get started. There are a lot of companies that will drop-ship products. You can go to Google and do a little bit of research.

However, what I would suggest is to choose a category.

You don't want to sell all kinds of products on your web site – you want to have a theme.

I would also recommend setting up a Yahoo store: **smallbusiness.yahoo.com/ecommerce/**

Yahoo provides you with a lot of tools that are easy to use and easy to set up. Everything is almost pre-done for you and all you have to do is just hire someone to design a simple Yahoo store and you're in business, probably within a month or so.

Yahoo Store Designers who I recommend are: **www.ydesigner.com** or **www.solidcactus.com**

This category has a few names you may have heard of: Amazon, Dell, iQVC, REI, Land's End, Garden.com, Wine.com, Fogdog – the list could go on and on. Obviously, there's huge profit potential here! But, as you can see, I've listed the 800lb. Gorillas of the Internet. If you're starting out, and you think e-commerce is the route for you, do your homework. The key is finding a niche that interests you where you can sell unique products that "slip under the radar" of the Big Boys.

This model is much more web-intensive, so it would be a good choice to understand how larger websites function. It would be a plus if you are comfortable writing and designing your own web pages, and if you have a good eye for attractive web design and layouts.

Also, if you enjoy, or have experience in retail merchandising, this would also help.

Proven Money-Making Model # 6 - eBook & Info-Marketing

Information marketing is my favourite business model because of its high profit margins. I love products and businesses that have high profit margins. Here's why: There will always be mistakes, and with higher profit margin items, there's more room for error. So even if I make a mistake, with high profit margins, I'm okay.

With low margin items, when you make a mistake, you're screwed.

Also, with high profit margin, that means I keep more of the money.

Let's say that I'm selling an e-book for $49.95. After I deduct the credit card fees, transaction fees, etc., my profit is still around 95%. That's very high compared to other products.

Plus, with a digital information product like an e-book, I don't have to ship anything. I don't have to stock anything; the customer simply buys the product, and they download it, so the business can be automated very easily. I don't need staff or to hire employees, so I like it much better.

ClickBank.Com – "No Merchant Account Needed and a Built-In Sales Staff!" If you're selling an e-book, you can use this site to sell it and you don't even need a merchant account! ClickBank will process your credit card payments and send you a cheque every two weeks.

In addition, you're tapping into an existing network of affiliate marketers who are looking for products to promote, so it's a very easy way to get started.

Always remember, when people go online, they're looking for information. They're looking for solutions to their problems. When they're looking for answers, do they want the answers fast, or do they want them slow? They want them fast, of course! They want it, and they want it now! They want instant gratification.

So an e-book and information marketing solves that problem.

Now, in my book, *Creativity Sucks!* (which you can order from Amazon.com), I talk about different ways that you can create information products quickly, even if you're not an expert in the subject matter.

Information marketing happens to be my specialty. It's the business model I have mastered.

I also want you to think outside the box when you think about information marketing. I'm not just talking about e-books. I'm talking about software, CDs, DVDs, tele-seminars, E-classes, seminars, and more. All of these things are considered to be information products. Information marketing is definitely my favourite business model and one you should highly consider.

Information Marketing is a billion-dollar industry. Think about it. At its basic level, a non-fiction printed book is an information product (although not a particularly profitable one most of the time).

People will buy information products to help them Make Money, Save Energy or Effort, Save Time, Be Healthier, Be More Spiritual, Be Popular, Be Prettier, Be Sexier, or Be Better at something.

You can sell Seminars, Tele-seminars, Newsletters, E-zines, Instructional DVD's, Books, Membership Sites, and Audio CD's to name a few different formats.

The profit potential is enormous because usually the production costs of info-products are usually low, and depending on the market, the prices you charge can be quite high.

Are you an expert in a particularly large field? People will pay you money to learn what you know if it will help them save the time, effort, or energy it would take to gather the information on their own.

In other words, if a person desperately wants to figure out "How To" do something, and you know "How To" do it, they will buy your information. This is a great field for any expert who is trying to leverage their knowledge.

For instance, if you are a Personal Fitness Trainer, there are only so many training clients that you can train in a day. Your income is topped out unless you raise your prices. However, let's say you have developed a knack for marketing your Personal Training to a wealthy clientele. There are plenty of trainers all around the country who would love to learn how you get those wealthy clients so easily. You could create an information product and sell it to other trainers, teaching them your system. This can leverage your specialized knowledge without adding time to your already busy schedule.

Proven Money-Making Model # 7 – Membership Site

A membership site is a very good business model because it provides you with recurring revenue. A membership site also allows you to build a community of loyal customers and, at the same time, if you have a forum, you can get to know them, find out what they're looking for, and easily develop other back-end products and services to offer to your members.

You can easily create a membership to solve a particular problem for people, or for a specific group of professionals (e.g., real estate agents, mortgage brokers, or real estate investing).

On your membership site you can have articles, audio, video, directories, different tools, industry news, forums and more. The only difficult part of a membership site is that you need to have a lot of content initially. But once you have enough members, then it becomes a very powerful business model.

A membership program that I use personally is called Member Gate (**http://www.membergate.com**).

There are other programs out there, but this is the one I recommend.

Depending on the size of your niche and the perceived value of your information, a membership site can be a gold mine. For instance, I know of an information marketer who sells how-to marketing information to a particular niche in the insurance industry. He charges $297 a month to be a part of his membership site. In his case, he's the "top dog" marketing coach in an industry that has only 60,000 agents nationwide.

I don't know how many members he has, but if he had only 5% of this particular niche, that's 3000 agents, each paying $297 a month – a total of $891,000 a month!

Subscriptions can be charged monthly, quarterly or yearly, but monthly is most common. A lifetime membership is also an option, but only if you have strong back-end sales potential.

Combine Different Business Models To Multiply Your Profits

Obviously, there are a lot more than seven business models.

For example, say you just want to build up a site so you can sell it. You don't care about revenue, you just want to build up the site's popularity, build up the traffic, and then turn around and sell it to some big dumb company for a lot of money. There are many other business models that I just don't have time to cover.

But one thing I would suggest for beginners is to just pick one model – just one – and just run with it. It doesn't matter which one, just do whatever is a good fit for you.

You see, you have to pick a business model that fits with who you are, something that you're interested in, something that you're passionate about (and knowledgeable in would be ideal). Just pick one and just do it.

And once you're up and running, once it's making money and you're established, the next step I would recommend – and this is where it gets really exciting, where you start seeing your profit multiply exponentially – is when you start to combine different business models to accelerate your growth.

Let's say, for example, you have a Yahoo store selling pillows. Now let's say that you write an e-book on how to get better sleep that you sell on ClickBank. This way, you can actually cross-promote the two products.

The e-book gives you, the store owner, a lot more credibility because now people look at you as an expert on the subject. When someone buys your e-book, you can drive them back to your Yahoo store or your e-commerce site, and sell them your pillows.

And with people who buy your pillows, you can sell them your e-book and teach them how to get better sleep. Do you see how this will help you grow the business much faster?

When you combine these different business models, you then have a very solid Internet business.

But again, for beginners, I would recommend just picking one and running with it.

Once it's developed, making some money, and is more established, then you can combine these different business models and see your income grow.

A former college dropout, Dan "The Man" Lok transformed himself from a grocery bagger in a local supermarket to a multi-millionaire. Dan came to North America with little knowledge of the English language and few contacts. Today, Dan is one of the most sought-after business mentors on the Web, as well as the author of his new and up-coming book, *F.U. Money: Make As Much Money As You Damn Well Want And Live Your Life As You Damn Well Please.*

Dan has developed his "Passive Income Mentoring Program" to show people just like you how to create recurring revenue streams. To get started creating your own lucrative ongoing passive revenue stream, go here now to grab your spot and get Dan's help:

http://www.danlokmentoring.com

IF I COULD ONLY HAVE ONE WAY TO MARKET AND ADVERTISE MY BUSINESS, THIS WOULD BE IT

By Owen Garrett

Owen Garratt is one of those "Bigger than life" kind of guys. Owen is a new friend of mine I met in 2008 at a Kennedy marketing convention. What he had done to completely transform his "art" business through effective direct response marketing got him in front of the entire 1,000+ seminar group showcasing his success.

Whereas most artists are dead broke, Owen has created a <u>very</u> successful business for himself and his family. He drives hot cars, has lots of 'toys", travels a ton – and lives life on his own terms.

A lot of what he has accomplished is due to his great use of a company newsletter. So read and learn from his example, and see how this can be applied to <u>you</u>.

~ Dave Dubeau

The Single best thing I've ever done in business – ignoring it cost me <u>at least</u> 2 million dollars in lost profit!

I procrastinated on this forever, but when it finally penetrated our mental cement that it worked, in the first year that we did this, we boosted revenue *over $200,000.*

What if:

- You created a sense of belonging in your clients, so they feel like part of a selected group of special individuals who are protective of you, constantly spread the word about you, and drive right past your competition to get to you?
- You had a dead simple, automatic way of keeping in front of your clients and prospects without hassling them, without constantly pitching them, or without using the usual advertising that goes in one ear and out the other?
- Your clients actually looked forward to your communications, and miss them when they don't arrive?
- This was also the **cheapest** and single most effective way to deliver your message to your clients?

No, it's not magic beans, but it's deceptively simple.

It's the lowly company newsletter.

HOLD IT!

"Stop right there!" you're thinking. "Newsletters? Bah!"

There's a good number of you who I just lost because newsletters aren't "sexy" enough to keep you reading this, but I promise that if you'll ride this out, you'll hear stuff you've never heard before, and if you'll just be open to the possibilities, the next year can be the best year you've ever had.

Why should you give a hoot about me and what I'm going to share with you?

My name is Owen Garratt, but you may know me as The Pencilneck ®. I've been an award-winning best selling artist for almost 15 years. Along with my wife Karla (henceforth known as The Colonel), we own Jackson's Extraordinary Custom Framing ™ in Spruce Grove, Alberta, and while there's obvious overlap, we run them as two distinct, if related, businesses. I'm in the top 1% of best selling artists in the world, and Jackson's is the highest volume retail custom picture framer in Canada.

And the biggest single boost we've ever given our businesses was getting serious about customer retention.

Everyone knows we need to keep in touch – it's the single biggest reason clients stop doing business with us: out of sight, out of mind. Don't fall into the lazy man's trap of "oh, they know where we are, when they need us, they'll come to us".

Not in this day and age, bubba.

EVERY business, no matter how successful and popular, has a certain amount of "client attrition", that is, you can't keep all of them happy all of the time.

Clients move away, they die, they have no further use for your goods or services, their brother-in-law got into your industry and they feel obligated to help him out, etc.

Even if you're doing everything right, you're losing customers every year, and it's not even your fault!

And let's be dirt honest here, nobody, I mean *nobody,* does a top-notch job of keeping in touch with clients. We all mean to, but c'mon, we're all too busy trying to keep a dozen balls in the air at a time to just "keep in touch" (whatever that means).

Some of us try to compensate with a basket of fruit at Christmas or a "customer appreciation event", and that's nice, but you know way deep down that it's not exactly efficient, even if you could measure it, which you can't.

We've all seen the stats of what it costs to get a new customer versus keeping an existing one, so why do we seem to be willing to throw any amount of money out the door to try and rope in a steady stream of new business, yet do nothing to keep the ones we've already made happy?

Personally, I think that it's because there's no newsletter sales rep.

Think about it, if there was somebody plopped down in front of you who could make all your customer retention concerns go away, you'd push over as much gold as you could if he could just "handle it".

Well, the good news is that there's a lot more help to do this than you may think.

So before we get too far along, let's just rip the band-aid off and address the most common excuses businesspeople have for not giving newsletters a fair shake:

It doesn't apply to my business

Respectfully, I suggest that you're just not thinking about it with an open mind. I'm an artist, but I've seen spectacular newsletters from all kinds of businesses, including chiropractors, financial planners, auto mechanics, and even a high-end pizza place.

I contend that it really doesn't matter what kind of business you're in: B2B, B2C, retail, medical practice, goods, services, wholesale, you name it. AND your business could and should use a newsletter not just to keep the business you have, but to grow as well.

All business boils down to people talking to people. Period. Even the eggheads and bean counters amongst us still prefer The Human Touch, even if it's only as a means of accountability and reassurance.

I'm no good at writing/ I don't like writing/ I flunked remedial English

Who cares? My official trick to writing boils down to this: write exactly as you speak, and if you wouldn't say it, don't write it. And don't try to be something you're not. If you stink at telling jokes, don't try to be funny in print.

I've got no time

Nobody does. I've got my art business, a gallery, a direct mail division, I'm finishing my first book, we're in pre-production for a reality show in the U.S., I'm recording a soundtrack album for the TV show, I need to travel like crazy, my sons are 4 and 6, and somehow I have to find time to draw too. And then there's my daily dose of *Seinfeld*, *The Simpsons*, and *The Food Network*.

But I'm able to produce 3 newsletters each month. How?

Keep reading…

It's too hard to come up with stuff each month

We'll talk about this too…

I'm just starting and/ or I have no list to send a newsletter too

Securing the full name and address of every prospect you meet is VITAL – we call it "Full Contact Marketing" at the gallery, and I'll show you how we built an instant list of over 1200 names overnight.

I'm broke! I can't afford to lick stamps!!!

Sure, there's some setup costs to doing a newsletter, but if you're just starting out you can print them on demand on your $99 home printer, and if you've only got $15 to market with today, you can still send out 25 newsletters…and do it again tomorrow.

How can you market for less than that?

I already send out email "newsletters" to my customers

Phffhft…how's that working out? I thought so.

Spam filters are picking out almost half of those emails. Emails have NO intrinsic value, they don't get passed around, they have to read it at the computer, and if you think that people are printing them out, you're delusional.

Emails are more efficient, but they're not nearly as effective. There's a huge difference.

I'm not saying stop emails if you've got some weird voodoo going on and you're actually getting <u>transactions</u> through email marketing – and I mean actual cash in the till, not just comments and "feedback" (ever try taking feedback to the bank? You can't pay a mortgage with slaps on the back. I've tried it).

If you've managed to make emails pay, keep doing it…but you still need a paper newsletter too.

NINE Reasons you need to do a newsletter NOW!

1. **It keeps you "Front of Mind"**
    Our ability to sell to clients doesn't necessarily synch up with our prospect's ability to do business with us.

    Everyone's had the experience of looking at a catalogue and saying to themselves, "I've GOT to get this!" And usually you have a small reason that you can't call right that second: You don't have your credit card at hand, you need to check the size or colour you need, you're not sure how many you need, you've got to check with so-and-so, you're short on time but you'll do it after lunch, etc.

    Then what happens?

Right, life gets in the way. You have every intention of ordering whatever that was, but before you know it, the phone's been ringing off the wall, your chickens get dandruff, pirates have been spotted in the West Edmonton Mall, you've got to caddy the kids around four nights a week, and before long that catalogue item is a distant memory, usually forgotten about until it's time to clean out the stacks of old printed matter and you accidently run across it again.

Newsletters Make Your Customers Remember You

I'd love to sell my limited edition prints of golf scenes year-round, but the fact is that the surge in demand is from March to August. But my Pencilneck ® newsletter lands on their desk monthly, and when The Boss sends word that it's time to pick up something for the company golf tournament, my stuff is pretty dashed fresh in their mind, as opposed to the scratched head and "we had something neat we were going to use this year...what was it?"

2. Efficiency

No matter how you slice it, newsletters are the most efficient way to market.

- They provide a superb return on investment
- They're easy to systemize so it happens automatically
- They can start small, but there's no limit on how big you can take it.
- You can do it on your own computer while you watch old M.A.S.H. reruns, you can outsource it, you can purchase "off the shelf" templates, and once you've got it down, your staff can take it and run (you don't think I actually stuff envelopes, do you?!?)

3. Hypeless communication

It allows us to keep in touch without being hypey and having them feel that they're being pitched all the time.

I contend that this is even more effective than all this "permission based marketing" hooey that's fadding around. Opt-in forms, double opt-in forms, and all the rest of that stuff is lousy positioning, and it creates a naggling little hassle that your clients need to go through so you can send them information. Bah! And even when you've got permission to market to someone, you can't all suddenly flood them with spam and pitch the tar out of them. You still need to treat your communication with your clients and prospects with a degree of respect for their time and still run a profitable business.

Do a great newsletter. It's part gossip column, part "what's new?", part "how to", and hopefully, interesting in a way that helps drive business to you.

It's not that far removed from that crazy uncle every family has that sends those terrific Christmas letters out… everyone reads them.

4. Stickyness

When you do it right, your clients look forward to your newsletters, and I doubt very highly that they look forward to any of your other advertising, do they? Newsletters become a bond between you and your clients, almost like a beloved character in a fiction series does over time.

They miss you when you're gone.

5. Mileage

Pass along. It's common that newsletters get passed from person to person (so allow multiple subscribers in one business if they want). This means that if your contact person leaves, you still have a presence with people in that company.

We even have a shocking number of clients who put our newsletters in a binder and leave them by their front desk!

6. Insane Profitability

It's the best, most profitable marketing I've ever done, and when I miss an issue, my numbers drop. I know of no other medium that can get me so much for so little. Yes, I'm counting Google Adwords too.

7. Maximum Positioning

This may be more advanced, but newsletters allow you to project the image you WANT the clients to have of you and your business. Are you a little schlub out in the boondocks who has to chase raccoons out every morning because your office is a rundown fishing shack? While I'd advise against pretending you're something you're not (a multi-national conglomerate with a staff of thousands for instance), you can still whack up your image a bit in the newsletter.

And much like authoring a book, it allows you to position yourself as an industry expert.

8. Recyclability

Here's a red-hot tip: Use previous newsletter articles for blog posts, and vice versa!

9. Scalability

Here's a major benefit: You can start small and pump them out on your home printer, and as your business grows, you can get to the point where all you do is email a PDF of your newsletter to a mail house and they print it out and mail it for you! (HINT. Get to this level as fast as you can!)

How To Build a Mailing List...Fast!

No mailing list? Just getting stated? No problem. Here's what we did to get 1200 names on our gallery list in one weekend!

- We got a booth at a local chamber of commerce show.

- Then we had an awesome draw box prize.
    - Use a big sign. Our sign for the draw was bigger than the sign with our company name!
    - Don't get cheap here...make it irresistible. Our prize was a free portrait by Best Selling Artist Owen Garratt valued at $4800.
    - You'll want to make it something that you don't sell IN the booth. People are funny and a certain amount of them will put off buying because they might win the prize.

- We had our staff (The Groovy Framing Elves ™) pounce on everyone that came by and playfully drag them over to enter the draw.

- DON'T just leave the forms out for people to fill out themselves – you've got to be proactive about this!

- On the form, be sure to get full contact info, including phone, mailing address, email, etc.

- On the entry form, put this line in bold: "FILL THIS IN PROPERLY! INCOMPLETE FORMS ARE INVALID!!!" And you still have to tell them to fill it in completely too.

Even so, fully a third of the entries won't be as complete as you'd like.

- "Hold it!" you're thinking. "I've been to these shows, and most of the people there aren't what I'd called "qualified"".

Quite right. And here's how you manage that.

- Get two different coloured entry forms – one for qualified prospects, and one for unqualified prospects. As you chat to them, you can sort of tell who may or may not be reasonably able and/ or willing to use what you've got. As for the infirm, insane, or otherwise unsuitable, they get the other coloured entry form. Don't go crazy here, just photocopy a regular piece of paper split into 8 forms, and photocopy it onto coloured paper, then trim them to size.

- Don't get too nuts about trying to sort this; the point isn't to precision target the PERFECT prospect, it's to avoid waste by trimming the obvious ones out.

- Make the draw legit. Keep all of the entries – both the suitable and the unsuitable – in the bin. In fact, our first draw winner was one of the "unsuitables", but he didn't fill out his form completely, so he was ineligible.

- Voilà… an instant list! At the end of the show, we had over 1200 reasonably suitable prospects, and we were able to cull out ones that were unlikely to pop into our gallery and shove money at us.

- And our first issue was about the chamber of commerce show, and our grand prizewinner, etc.

- Now, don't be one of those people that reads that and says, "Yes, but I don't have a gallery, this'll never work for me". Adapt it to your business…figure it out!

Content: What to put in your newsletter…

This is The Big Hurdle for most businesses. "What the heck do I fill a newsletter with??!"

Goals for your newsletter:
- Positioning yourself as the expert
- Keeping in your clients' "front of mind"
- A call to action
- Touching your client base (we call it "dribbling on them")
- Ongoing client education

We have a "lead story", which is a sort of current events update, and then fill the rest of the newsletter with "monthly columns". These columns should compliment you and your business to the greatest extent possible.

Use some common sense here. If you can't cook or you're anorexic, then there's little use in putting recipes into your newsletter (maybe diet tips?). My personal story is of a gourmand, a musician, and a bookworm, so having recipes, music, book, and movie reviews make sense.

Three vital points:
- Include testimonials!!

- Include a customer of the month/ customer story wherever possible
- Include a monthly special...then advertise that special through other media too! Example: if you're having a Father's Day special, then advertise it everywhere, in your newsletter, newspaper ads, monthly statements, etc.

NOTE: My samples may not show all of these points as I sometimes put them in the cover letter or inserts...but they're always there!

You can see samples of my newsletter at:
www.pencilneck.com/newsletters

Other Ideas for Newsletter Content:
- Testimonials
- Movie reviews
- Tip of the month
- Crosswords or Sudoku
- Book reviews
- Music/ CD reviews
- Restaurant reviews
- Travel reviews
- Recipes
- Horoscopes
- Jokes
- This month in history
- Calendar of events
- Client of the month profile
- Staff member of the month profile
- Special offer of the month
- Trivia questions

- Related industry content
- Education about yours or related services
- Rants (careful though!)
- Business tips
- Household tips
- Family tips

Again, the majority of these columns can be done in one whack for the whole year, which saves TONS of time down the road…and don't forget to source things online!

The newsletter as a LEAD-GENERATING device?!?

A friend of ours, Rita Krause, owns and runs Mewassin Automotive Ltd near Wabamun, AB, and she uses newsletters as a lead generating device by using them as bulk mail (re: junk mail).

Rita's shop is out in the middle of nowhere, so she needs to get clients to drive way out to see her – there's no drive by traffic.

She sends out approximately 5000 flyers/ newsletters each month to postal codes in her service area, and the results have been spectacular. In the first seven months, she generated an additional $250,000, strictly by newsletters!

Also, Rita told me that this past February (2009) was the BEST February they've had in 22 years in business. How many other business can say that?

These newsletters are done very inexpensively as tri-fold flyers, printed black and white on coloured paper. There's a couple of points to mention specific to bulk newsletters:

We'll be implementing bulk newsletters for our gallery this spring, but we'll be keeping the content different from our existing client letters.

- These bulk newsletters can be more "salesy" – keep asking people to call or "pop in"
- Every issue needs an offer so you can keep track of the results
- Include a map to your business! This should be self-explanatory
- Full contact info. Again, but it's easy to miss

25 Tips for doing a red-hot newsletter...*FAST*

1. Do it once

Template it. The word documents in Windows have lots of great templates to fart around with (you Mac snobs must have an equivalent), and there's about a zillion available online.

Once this is done, you can just copy and paste each month's content and away you go.

2. Start as a One Sheet

We do our newsletters as a 11" x 17" that gets folded in half to make four 8 ½" x 11" pages. If that's too much for you to start, you can begin with a single sheet of paper and print it two sides. Don't wait to be "perfect", just get it done!

3. Use free content

For our Jackson's Extraordinary Custom Framing ™ newsletter, The Colonel stuffs it with great content provided by the Professional Picture Framer's Association. The PPFA, (and your industry does too, just look) gets lots of content for its members to use in press releases, articles, etc, and it's FREE!

The Colonel scoops up content that relates to our business and ties in with whatever our monthly special event is.

For instance, if we're having Spring Cleaning event, the newsletter will run an article on how to clean framed art and how NOT to clean framed art. This ties elsewhere in the newsletter that Jackson's ™ Spring Cleaning Special is 25% off all cleaning and repairs: cracked glass, moisture damage, dinged frames, etc.

The article lists a myriad of problems that can happen with improperly stored and cleaned art. And we solve the problem dawning in their minds of "Egad! It needs cleaning but I don't want to screw it up!" by including a special offer to pop in and we'll handle it for them and they save 25% off.

If you Google "free articles", you'll find enough free content to last forever, and they explain the rules very plainly.

4. Do a year at a time

This was a big breakthrough for us: doing up a year's worth of articles at a time! It's way easier to sit down and push out 12 book reviews, or 12 movie reviews, or 12 recipes in an afternoon than to start each month from scratch.

By the second week of January each year, I have 85% of my year's articles written!

All that leaves is each month's lead article, and I can do that in a couple of hours.

5. Develop your character
This goes with positioning yourself. You need to think about character development, because that's what you are! Include little psychic "anchors" to help your clients fasten themselves to.

Calling my wife "the Colonel" was no accident; it was consciously thought out with her full participation. She even uses it in her email. (I had suggested The Warden, but she was cool to that idea!)

6. Quit screwing around with format!!!
You can spend months mucking around with this. Keep it simple, and get it done. Accept that changes will be inevitable, and fix it over the coming months if need be.

7. Use lots of pictures
It's kind of hard to overdo this. Pictures are vital; use them everywhere you can.

8. And make them action shots
Wherever possible, avoid the static "real estate agent" type of head shot, especially the ones with the head title. Gakkk! Pictures that look like you're doing something are intrinsically more interesting. Go to my website (**www.pencilneck.com/newsletter**) and look at the upper right and left header. On every single page or page refresh, two new photos appear…you'll get the idea.

9. Keep the fonts simple

The Colonel and I fight over this to no end. She wants flowery, decorative fonts, and she's of the opinion that you can't have too many fonts and would, I'm sure, use a different font for every single word.

Don't do that. We use Times New Roman for headlines, and Arial for body copy, with occasional bolds and italics for emphasis. They're the easiest to read and reproduce.

10. Color isn't all that important

If you're trying to save some bread to start, it's fine to go black and white.

11. Use coated paper

It makes a HUGE difference. We always use laser paper; the coating means we can use thinner paper while still having a nice look and feel.

12. Don't sacrifice content for logo and graphics

You need 'em, but they're secondary to content.

13. Get quotes

Get quotes from lots of printers, including Staples, OfficeMax, Office Depot, etc. There's more spread in prices than you think.

14. Print digitally first, then go offset

Digital printing just means using a computer and printer to print newsletters. Once you get past 24-36 newsletters, you'll want to stop doing them yourself. They just don't look as good, and the ink costs are atrocious.

The next step is to farm them out to a print shop.

There's a point when digitally printing is more expensive than traditional offset printing... and that's a happy day! Once you get to needing 2000+ a month, begin exploring having your newsletters done on a proper printing press.

15. Attach a cover letter

This gives it more of a personal touch – so address it to the person! Use Microsoft Word's mail merge function... it's a snap.

16. Soft sell

Use the cover letter and inserts to pitch; it comes off better and allows the newsletter to be about relationships, not just transactions.

17. Envelope VS self mailer

We prefer envelopes so we can include lots of sales materials, cover letters, price sheets, etc.

18. Be aspirational

They should want to be like you or take part in what you've got going on.

19. But don't be a braggart!

It's about them, not you.

20. Always write with contractions

It sounds much more conversational. 'there's", not 'there is". "I'm", not "I am", etc.

21. Speak Like The Queen

Whenever possible, use the Victorian "we" instead of "I". Otherwise you'll sound like an egomaniac... or Martha Stewart (same thing).

22. Read your newsletter out loud when proofing

Every time I proof it in my own head I miss scads of mistakes. And have someone else proof it aloud too.

23. Don't be boring

You can be dry as hell in real life, but in your marketing you need to be distinctive and have an aura of likeability.

24. Make it entertaining

Make it so good that they'd miss it if it didn't show up next month. This also helps to ensure that it gets passed around.

25. Full contact info

Everybody seems to skip this at least once. If you have clients coming to you, be sure to include a map to your business.

There you go – a full primer on how any business can successfully use newsletters to grow their business through lead generation, customer contact, and client retention.

I noticed an interesting thing when I committed to newsletters: I did okay for a month or two, but then I used up my "material" and I had nothing new to write about! It dawned on me that if I was going to have anything interesting to write about, then I'd better go do something interesting.

And a funny thing happened... my life became more interesting!

So take that as the Big Idea: A newsletter not only grows your business, but it can help to grow your life. Now go get 'em!

If you'd like to see some examples of how we do it, you can check out a couple of my newsletters and download PDFs on my website at **www.pencilneck.com/newsletter**

Owen Garratt, born in Regina SK has very quickly become a best selling artist and everyone's favourite Pencilneck®, while remaining a well kept secret. As Owen likes to put it, he's "... *completely unencumbered by formal instruction*" and his art is strictly black and white, due to a degree of colour blindness that leaves him unable to see certain pigments.

He has been a full time artist from his very first drawing in 1995 and is in the top 1% of best selling artists around the world.

In 2003, Owen and his wife Karla Elder opened Sketchie's Gallery, later changed to Jackson's Extraordinary Custom Framing, and already enjoys a worldwide reputation as 'The Leader in Preserving Memories" ™, and in 2009 Jackson's is on target to become the highest volume retail custom picture framer in Canada.

In perhaps the biggest development in his career to date, Owen also is starring in a television series about his life and art that's currently in development for one of the major cable networks in the United States, and his test footage won 1st prize at the LATV Festival!

In addition to being a World Class artist, Owen is a former full time freelance drummer, an avid bookworm and writer, an intrepid adventurer, a great outdoors loving, husband, father and all round Good Joe.

FREE Gift Offer! Get over $595.00 in additional marketing and business building special reports, audio CD's and DVD's mailed right to your door. See page 271 for complete details, or visit: **www.ResultsEnterprises.com/gift.html**

SHOW & TELL TO GROW YOUR BUSINESS: EVENTS

By Dave Dubeau

One of the fastest (and potentially most enjoyable) ways to grow your business is by putting on "events" for customers and prospects. When I'm talking about events I mean several different things:

1. Promotional events
2. Client appreciation events
3. Seminars/ Public speaking

Let's begin the discussion with the most common one that we are familiar with: **Promotional Events** can be tied in with a Big Sale of some sort.

So instead of just having a boring old "sale", you turn it into an "experience". For example, a car dealership might have a Sale and bring in a petting zoo for the kids, rent big inflatable toys for them to play in, provide hot dogs & pop etc. It gives people a reason to come in <u>besides</u> just seeing a bunch of vehicles for sale.

The goals are multiple. First of all, you want to attract a bunch of potential car buyers. Secondly, you want to create "buzz" and get a lot of people in general to come out. Some may turn into car buyers. Thirdly, you want to create a "warm fuzzy" feeling in people. So after they come to your event, when they <u>are</u> ready to buy another car, you will be the one who pops into their mind first. (It works <u>much</u> better if you somehow capture their contact info & follow up with them consistently). Fourth, you want to create a "family" get together. So both Mom and Dad come out. That means you have both decision makers there; this = easier sale.

OK. You don't have a car dealership – still works! Any business can do this kind of thing – you think of something fun to base it on. Your sale & some entertainment & some food & some fun & anything to capture contact info of new people to follow up with (a draw is great for this).

But what if I have a business that doesn't lend itself to "sales"? (For example, professional practices – you probably won't see a dentist doing 2 for 1 root canals will you?) You can still make this work very well for you with client/ patient/ customer appreciation events. So in this case you do a lot of the same as with the mentioned event. You create a good reason for people to come in to have some fun. Anniversary of your business; your birthday; or Holiday of some sort etc. But in this case you aren't really pro-moting this hard to "cold" prospects – you are promoting it to your current and past customers, and you are encouraging them to bring their friend(s) with them.

Think of the Remax balloon example: Customer prospects get to go for a ride in the balloon when it comes through town. That's an event.

Wine and cheese get-togethers are great. In fact, you can work together with other non-competing businesses with similar target interests and get twice the bang for your buck! They invite their people & you invite yours.

So let's look at our car dealer example again. Maybe they team up with a high end clothing store and a jeweller to hold a client appreciation fashion show at the dealership! All 3 companies invite their customers (+ perhaps a friend) to this "exclusive" event. That in itself creates <u>demand</u> for the next one – people "want" to be invited – so they end up purchasing from you, basically to be on the list.

So let's say each business gets 30 people to come out. This means there are 90 people in total – and about 60 "new" prospects for each company <u>plus</u> more business from each business current customer.

This doesn't even have to involve a "pitch" for any potential products. All you do is "feature" them. This <u>works</u>.

Yeah Dave, great, but I have a "boring business". I'm a (fill-in-the-blank). I think this works for <u>any</u> business. Let's look at a roofing construction and another example.

Why not host a BBQ at a home where you have just done a job? Have the home owner invite all their friends and family over – you put it on – and your business gets featured or better yet join up with their landscaper, pool company, hot tub company, pool table seller, whatever renovation etc., and split the costs. Also, if you do it right you could probably promote this to your lists and the home owners would be happy to be featured as the "perfect feature home" because this = huge ego stroke for them.

I've heard Dan Kennedy talk about an insurance agent who puts on a big birthday party for himself every year. He rents out a restaurant for the day, providing free food (and drink) for his customers and encouraging them to bring friends.

He gets perched on a Big "throne" with a crown and a couple of pretty assistants and people parade by him giving him "prank" gifts! The first year he had 50-60 people come out. Now it has become a noon-midnight extravaganza with over 1,000 people coming through!

It has reached the point where this is the <u>only</u> marketing this fellow does during the entire year. And now he doesn't really even follow up with people; they just call him wanting to update or get insurance. And about 2/3 of the people who come through are new prospects. I can't think of a much more fun way of doing business – can you?

A good friend of mine, Des Regier, from Trade Exchange Canada (a Barter company in Kelowna, BC), holds <u>monthly</u> meet and greets for his clients & prospects. This is really smart because every month he holds one at a different client's business location. All of the attendees enjoy some complimentary wine & cheese. They get to mingle & network. The "host" business gets featured and talks about what they do. Des also gets to promote whatever is going on with his company and talk with prospects who are very "warm". It's a real win-win-win, and he does it every single month. Twelve times a year…Smart!

Again, I firmly believe that this can be done for any business.

Now we come up to the next thing on our list – and probably the scariest one for a lot of people. And that is…

Public Speaking & Seminars

Public speaking is one of the fastest and most effective ways to grow your business. Why? For a couple of reasons:

1. **Credibility:** We've all heard the stats about the fear of public speaking being greater than the fear of death. If you do not suffer from this fear and are able to speak in front of a group, you are instantly respected by a lot of the people in the audience.

   There is also a lot of inferred expertise placed on you. If you get up and give a talk on your subject, you are automatically assumed to be an expert on it.

2. **Leverage:** This respect and credibility, combined with the info you are presenting to a group of people (instead of one-to-one), creates massive leverage for you.

   Now people will seek you out, and they are pre-sold about working with you.

CASE STUDY # 1: Financial Planner

My financial planner acquaintance, Les Consenheim, here in Kamloops, puts on seminars 2-3 times a year. He'll often have the "big wigs" from the investment he is marketing come out and do a presentation on it.

Again, he focuses on his current and past clients, and encourages them to bring friends. That's all he does. And the nice thing here is he doesn't have to do the presentation! His "agents" do it.

CASE STUDY # 2: Door Knob Ads – Business Builder Workshops

When I was in the advertising business selling door knob ads I was tired of meeting with prospects one-on-one. It seemed like a real time waster to me.

So I partnered up with 2 other non-competing businesses, and we put on a series of "Business Builder Workshops" in 3 local towns. We pooled our resources, each putting in $1,000 for marketing. I got the local papers and radio stations to be "sponsors" (and that translated into 2+1 ads with them). We did direct mail to the local chamber of commerce and each one of us promoted the events to our "house" clients.

Events + Public Speaking = Easy Sales + Big $

We got an average of 50 people out to each event – and they were all local, small business owners (our target market). Each one of us gave a 45-minute presentation ending with a pitch for our products/ services.

For me, the bottom line was that I did 3 presentations and sold $23,000 worth of advertising to warm-eager prospects. To do that same volume of business, I probably would have had to do 50-60 one-on-one presentations. My friend, Des Regier, signed on 19 new members to his Trade Exchange Co.

CASE STUDY # 3: Cooperation With A Local Non-Profit Organization

I did something similar recently when launching my BC Profit$ membership program. But this time, instead of being a "free" to attend event, we charged money for it and had all of the funds collected donated to the local Food bank.

This allowed us not only to support a very worthy local charity, but also to get big discounts on advertising. It also provided us with a cause to support.

"Dave, it all sounds good...but I'm scared to death of public speaking!"

Well, if you are willing to stretch your comfort zone a bit, it's really not that tough. However, you want to do it right. That means that if you are a novice to public speaking, get some quality training first.

I always recommend Toast Masters. I was a part of that group for 18 months, and it was great. You learn public speaking in a completely supportive environment and you take baby steps to begin with. Nothing too scary.

Toast Masters groups are in most communities, and you can get contact info by visiting **www.toastmasters.org**

I've also heard very good reviews about Dale Carnegie training as well. I haven't done it myself, however. I think they are much more intense, short term programs. **www.carnegietraining.ca**

Holding events & public speaking is definitely a short cut to new business for you. Even if you are a shy wallflower of a person, you can take advantage of this. Hold a client/ customer/ patient appreciation event to just mix & mingle.

It will give people some nice "warm fuzzies" about you and your company and lead to more business.

If you are still nervous about doing it alone, or if you prefer some company, then do something with some other non-competing business with similar target customers. Share your customers and attract their friends!

And if you are really aggressive, do both of those. Hold events in your business and take your show on the road (figuratively speaking) with live seminars.

Become the recognized center and expert in your field locally. Your credibility will grow, you will be seen as the expert, you may become a local "celebrity", and most importantly, you will make more money.

That is how you can "show & tell" to grow your business. No matter what your business is!

Dave Dubeau began his infatuation with marketing while living in San Jose, Costa Rica. By learning and implementing effective direct response marketing, he was able to take his start-up company from the bottom of the pack to the top three (with over 50 competitors) in 2.5 years.

Upon returning to Canada in 2003 with his Costa Rican wife, Susy, and their two kids, Amy and Andrew, Dave continued to put his marketing skills to good use – first in the field of "Creative Real Estate Investing", where he did "18 flips in 18 months", then with an advertising business, and later as a marketing consultant.

Dave really came into his own as a bona-fide marketing expert when he began working with "Canadian Rich Dad", Darren Weeks. Together they created the *Fast Track Inner Circle* membership program, and Dave eventually became the "Marketing Guy" for Darren's Fast Track group of companies. Dave began a whole new marketing focus for the companies, helped to quadruple the database from 15,000 to over 60,000 event attendees, and helped the companies to grow to $100M in gross annual sales.

Dave is a firm believer in on-going education and he invests tens of thousands of dollars a year going to a variety of marketing conferences, seminars and mastermind group meetings (many through the prestigious Glazer-Kennedy organization).

Dave's company is appropriately called **Results Enterprises Inc**. and is based out of Kamloops, British Columbia in Canada.

If you would like more information about Dave Dubeau and what he does, please visit **www.ResultsEnterprises.com**

FREE Gift Offer! Get over $595.00 in additional marketing and business building special reports, audio CD's and DVD's mailed right to your door. See page 271 for complete details, or visit: **www.ResultsEnterprises.com/gift.html**

Notes & Thoughts!

A BRIGHT
IDEA

Notes & Thoughts!

A BRIGHT IDEA

CONCLUSION

Congratulations and Thank you very much for investing your time, attention and consideration by reading this book.

You may very well be feeling a little overwhelmed right now – as there is a lot of great information and fantastic marketing ideas, tips and strategies in this book. To begin with, I'd suggest you pick the TOP 3 items that resonated with you the most.

Once you have chosen those Top 3, then pick the one that would have the biggest immediate effect on your situation right now, and begin working with that first.

Do something – anything to get moving on that idea today. Do more research about it. Make a call. Check out some websites. Write an e-mail. Brainstorm the idea with a colleague. Write out an action plan around the idea – but take some ACTION on it immediately.

Of course, if you would like any further assistance on that particular topic from the author of the chapter you read about it in – then please feel free to contact them directly. They will be pleased to hear from you – and make sure you tell them you read about them in this book (so that they will give you priority treatment).

For more information about Results Enterprises and what we do, please visit our website at: **www.ResultsEnterprises.com**

Cheers, and start Making Money with YOUR Marketing!

Dave Dubeau

FREE: Over $595.00 of Cutting Edge Business Reports, CD's and Newsletters!

**Copy this page and FAX this form to: 1-888-851-8890
or visit www.ResultsEnterprises.com/gift.html**

_____ YES Dave! I want to take you up on This FREE Business Info Package worth $595.80

Here's what you'll get:

How To Quickly And Easily Create A Business Card That Sells. Special Report – Brandon Roe. Value $39.00

Forbidden Psychological Tactics – Dan Lok. Value: $49.00

2 Months of the FTIC Membership + Bonus (New members only). Value: $113.90

The Greatest Success Secret in the World – Dan Lok. Value: $49.00

How to Work Less and Make a Lot More Money! Audio CD. Dan Lok. Value: $39.00

The 7 Keys to Creating Wealth in Canada. Audio CD "Canadian Rich Dad" Darren Weeks with Dave Dubeau. Value $39.95

"How to Get Rich in Canada" DVD "Canadian Rich Dad" Darren Weeks. Value: $49.95

"How I Created a $35,783.15/month Joint Venture from Scratch...& You Can Too!" Workbook & Auido CD package. Dave Dubeau. Value: $97.00

J.V. Bootcamp DVD by Robin J. Elliott. Value: $89.00

How to Recession Proof Your Business Right Now. Special Report by Neil Godin. Value: $30.00

To take advantage of this FREE Business Info Package you only pay a one-time charge of $14.95 (+gst) to cover postage (and this is for everything – the package, and the 2 month trial membership).

Then, after the FREE 2 months of receiving the Fast Track Inner Circle (FTIC) Membership benefits, I will automatically charge you the lowest price that I offer FTIC membership, only $39.97 (+gst) a month. And here's the best part. If during the FREE 2 months, or anytime after that, you want to cancel your Membership, simply give us a call at 1-866-680-3842 or fax us a note at 1-888-851-8890 and my office will STOP charging your credit card immediately. No hassles. No hard feelings. You must be completely satisfied. If not, I want you to cancel your Membership.

NAME:_____

BUSINESS NAME:_____

ADDRESS (No P.O. Boxes)_____

CITY:_____ Prov._____ P.Code_____

EMAIL: _____

CREDIT CARD ☐ Visa ☐ MasterCard ☐ American Express

CREDIT CARD#:_____ EXP.DATE:___/___/

SIGNATURE: _____ DATE _____

OR GO ONLINE TO:

www.ResultsEnterprises.com/gift.html